SAKA SAKA

Adventures in African Cooking, South of the Sahara

ANTO COCAGNE & ALINE PRINCET

Photography: Aline Princet
Design: Isabelle Brouant

Wax prints on cover page and chapter opening pages:
SONNA INTERNATIONAL

Interlink Books

An imprint of Interlink Publishing Group, Inc.
Northampton, Massachusetts

FOREWORD

. . . .

ADVENTURES IN AFRICAN COOKING

For several years now, Western society has shown increasing interest in African culture, driven in particular by the valuable work of African artists across a multitude of genres. This is seen through the rise in contemporary art exhibitions, literature, fashion, and decor (like beautiful wax-print fabrics), films (including *Black Panther*, the 2018 Marvel blockbuster), and more African musicians in the limelight—a new Black power, so to speak, that transcends boundaries. So why is African culture largely missing from the Western culinary canon, considering the intercontinental gastronomic explosion of recent years? Food is also a key part of African culture, but the continent's rich culinary heritage is grossly underappreciated here.

As a photographer specializing in the culinary field, I have been illustrating works related to global cuisines for years, but never from Sub-Saharan Africa. I was excited to showcase this often-neglected cuisine by **placing it squarely in the spotlight and dispelling some of the deeply rooted yet unfounded misconceptions** associated with it. I have been privileged to enjoy African meals that were both delightful in taste and also in the moments in which they were shared. This work is more than a cookbook because it is not simply a collection of recipes.

Just like these wonderful meals, I wanted this book to be a **lively celebration of conviviality, generosity, and cultural wealth**, a beautiful contemporary work, far from ethno-folkloric clichés, but at the same time firmly guided by African roots and voices. And given that it is a book about sharing and cooking, I cannot help but quote Epicurus: "We should look for someone to eat and drink with before looking for something to eat and drink." This is why I invited **personalities with Sub-Saharan African heritage and diverse backgrounds to dine at this "table":** an artist, a writer, musicians, a choreographer, and a fashion designer, all of whom are champions of their cultures. **You will encounter each person through portraits and interviews as they describe** their favorite dishes and, **importantly, the sensory experiences associated with them.** Cooking, just like a song or a tune, can transport us back to an exact time and place, to a specific emotion ... and this is a universal feeling. Taste can bring back childhood memories, especially for those who are far from home and their culture.

It was vivacious journalist, Soro Solo, already active in changing the perception of Africa in the West, who was the first to enthusiastically accept my invitation to "come to the party" (referring to his former show *Le Bal de L'Afrique Enchantée* on France Inter, see p. 40).

But before even setting the table, someone had to excel in making the meal. Chef Anto's **vibrant personality, enthusiasm, and wealth of knowledge, together with her innovative and creative cuisine that remains firmly grounded in her roots,** made her the obvious person to do this. She is a dedicated ambassador of Sub-Saharan African cuisines and culture.

This book is named *Saka Saka* after the cassava leaf dish that is a staple across the African continent, appearing in a variety of different forms with different names (see p. 96). The adventurous spirit of the book is reflected in the traditional wax-print imagery chosen to illustrate it. It is cheerful and playful, yet sophisticated, with an individualistic tone that is conveyed in the artist features in particular.

This book aims to modestly **pay tribute to many food-loving Africans and reveal a little piece of this diverse, vibrant, and epicurean continent.** Whether you are from the diaspora, of African heritage, or just love Africa and African culture, I hope this book will bring you joy and make your mouth water! So I say welcome, or *bonne arrivée*, as I have often been greeted in Benin. Enjoy these tastes from Africa!

Aline Princet

. . . .

BASES AND APPETIZERS

CONT

MAINS

THE CUISINES OF AFRICA

Africa is a continent made up of 54 sovereign states. Straddling the equator, it encompasses a great number of climates: equatorial in the center and near coastal areas; wet tropical on the fringes of the equatorial region; tropical temperate with a dry climate and dry winter in a large part of southern Africa; semi-arid and arid in the north with high temperatures and very low rainfall; temperate near the Mediterranean with hot and dry summers and cool and wet winters.

This diversity in climates is an initial indicator of the diversity of produce, and consequently cuisines found in Africa. While we often talk about African cuisine, it would be more insightful to refer to the "cuisines of Africa." Even though the basics are often similar, **there are actually as many African cuisines as there are African countries, cultures, and dialects.** And while the Maghreb region is the most well-known from a culinary perspective, the Sub-Saharan region is yet to be recognized.

Traditionally, the various African cuisines mainly use local produce like fruits, grains, and vegetables, with very little meats, since the majority of people (with the exception of the most well off) don't have the means to eat meat and fish every day.

African cuisines are often mislabeled as too oily, too spicy, too rich, too strong smelling or criticized for being served up in a slapdash manner ... But if you are able to enjoy a French foie gras, delight in a good homemade mayonnaise or hollandaise sauce, savor a smelly blue cheese, or eat your sushi with wasabi, then **you will be able to appreciate the varied and tasty dishes that come from the cradle of humanity.** Besides, a dish with spices and a spicy dish are two completely different things, and you now have no excuse not to try them because, in Africa, we can also do "chile on the side!"

And finally, African cuisines are **varied and healthy, plus they're often gluten-free, vegetarian, and sometimes vegan.**

So, jump in and discover the best recipes that the colorful and delicious cuisines of Sub-Saharan Africa have to offer!

Anto Cocagne

In my opinion, a cookbook must be useful. If the recipes are too complicated to make, then I would have missed the mark as an author. My goal is to make African recipes accessible to everyone and not to discourage beginners. I therefore decided not to include some recipes that I consider to be too laborious. This is true of ndolé, the national dish of Cameroon, typically from the coastal province, which was previously reserved for important ceremonies as its preparation required at least a day's work. This is mostly due to the very bitter leaves that take a long time to prepare in order to be edible.

Anto Cocagne was born in France while her parents were students, but grew up in their home country of Gabon. At the age of 20, she returned to France to study cooking, much to her father's disappointment. But the government of Gabon refused to give her a grant to study: "All girls know how to cook, why do you need to go to France for that?" they asked. But Anto held her ground.

Cooking is Anto's passion—she was already selling homemade pastries to the students at her high school and all around her neighborhood. Her parents believed in her and let her go. They made the right decision.

After completing a vocational certificate in culinary arts and a bachelor's degree in food service, Anto went to Paris to study at École Grégoire-Ferrandi, an internationally recognized school of culinary arts. There she specialized in event cuisine and completed a qualification with a focus on catering.

a modern spin. Pan-African? Yes, it was important for her to showcase African produce rather than individual countries because, as she has always said, "the borders between the countries in Africa were not chosen by Africans but imposed on us."

Neither clients nor chefs in the West are usually familiar with Sub-Saharan cuisine. "People tend to eat out at Japanese or Indian restaurants. But who goes to restaurants serving Sub-Saharan African cuisine? Still mainly members of the African community," says Anto regrettably. Her idea was to rework traditional African dishes with a careful selection of spices and showcase their beauty.

Anto Cocagne puts her talent to work in many ways, including as a home chef, consultant helping restaurants revamp their menus, and recipe coordinator for *Afro Cooking*, the leading African cooking magazine.

TWO COUNTRIES, ONE CUISINE

CHEF

Anto alternated her studies with internships at the Carlton Cannes hotel, with French chef Éric Pras at his restaurant Meilleur Ouvrier de France, and with some of the biggest names in Parisian catering. Following this, she spent a year in the United States working as a sous-chef at a Hilton hotel in South Carolina.

With all this experience behind her, Anto hoped to return to work in Gabon ... but she found the reception was icy. Restaurants in Libreville preferred to have male and European chefs in their kitchens. So, Anto headed back to France, where she started her business with a bold ambition: she wanted to make traditional pan-African cuisine, but with

And because credibility is always elusive for a female chef, and especially one of color, in 2018 Anto decided to take part in the exclusively female Golden Spoon Awards. It was a great success! Anto was one of the six finalists selected and then she was also awarded the Eugénie Brazier Special Prize for her creativity.

Since 2019, Anto has been the presenter of the *Rendez-vous* program on French television channel Canal+. In each episode she takes viewers on a tour of an African country through its cuisine. It's an opportunity to introduce the general public to the tastes and smells of Africa's varied culinary cultures.

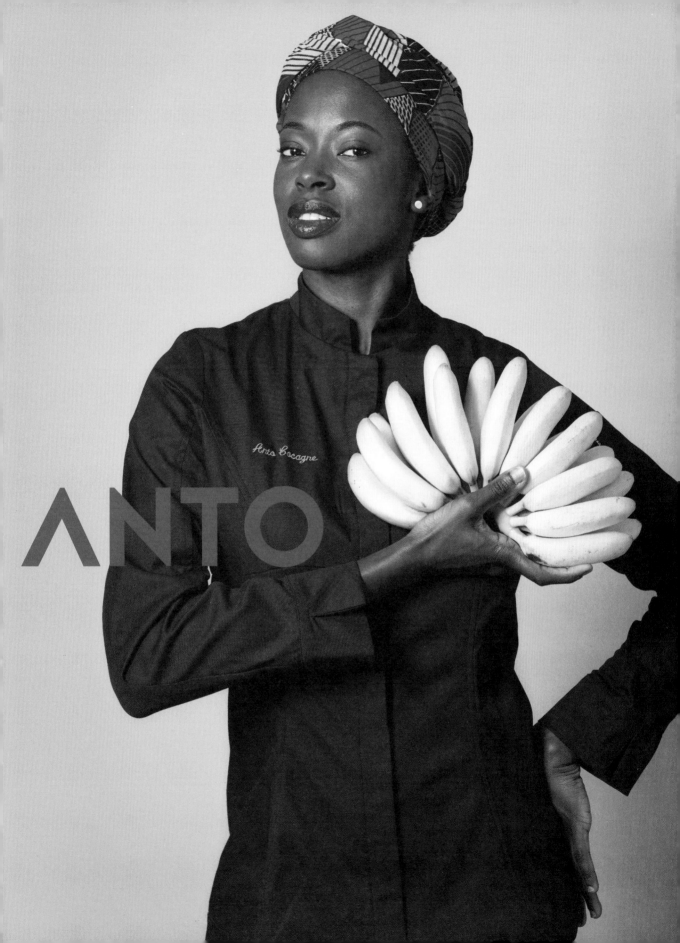

TASTES FROM AFRICA

To understand how African cuisines have evolved, we first need to look back at the continent's history.

What did people eat in Africa before colonization? It's a difficult mystery to solve. Ancient Africa did not leave any written texts, and because recipes were handed down orally, many have unfortunately been buried with the ancestors.

In 5000 BC, there was a series of migrations of the Bantu people on the continent. The Bantus were constantly on the move, taking their recipes with them and adapting them systematically to the local environment where they were. In addition, the Arab presence in Africa and the ensuing spread of Islam to these regions pre-dates the European presence. This is how the Arab-Berbers brought couscous to West Africa. The Arabs starting trading with the East, which probably contributed to the introduction of several spices.

Produce such as tomatoes, cassava, potatoes, sweet potatoes, squash, zucchini, beans, corn, peanuts, chile, sweet peppers, cacao, vanilla, and pineapple all have American origins. These products were therefore unknown to Africans and Europeans before the 15th century.

Lastly, Africa prior to the colonial era was made up of kingdoms. When Europe divided up the continent following the Berlin Conference in 1884–85, the empires were split up. This is why some dishes are very similar, but differ depending on the country or ethnic group.

While some tasks such as hunting were reserved for men, cooking was above all women's business. Even now, there are still tribes where a man is not allowed to set foot inside a kitchen. Recipes are handed down orally, from mother to daughter. And if a woman only has sons, she will hand down her recipes to her nieces or her daughters-in-law.

Whether it be for festive or everyday dishes, this book is an ode to the tastes of Sub-Saharan Africa.

PRINCIPLES AND TRADITIONS

Before going any further, here are a few basic principles you should know:

• **Eating with your hands is completely normal and not at all primitive.** Western countries are often so conditioned otherwise that they see eating with your hands as dirty and inelegant.

Studies have shown, however, that eating with your hands is actually better for your health because it forces you to eat more slowly. There is something sacred about eating like this—it's a way of connecting with the food you are eating. And, to be honest, it's more fun!

- **Meals are a time for sharing, talking, and meeting together.** Parents and children eat together. When there are guests, adults and younger people eat separately, but meals remain convivial. In the West, it is unusual to drop by uninvited to someone's house, but in African cultures people always cook more in case someone turns up unannounced.

- **Meal frequency is variable,** between one and three meals per day, depending on the family's financial means and the resources they have available. Meals are traditionally structured around a main and often communal dish that is usually prepared in plentiful quantities. These days, some people try to follow the pattern of appetizer followed by a main dish, and then a dessert, but it's not something that is part of African cultures. The meal usually ends by serving one or more fresh fruits. Snacks are eaten at afternoon tea time for school kids, and after leaving the office for workers. Barbecues are popular in the evening, accompanied by beer or local drinks.

- With only a few exceptions, **you can't buy canned or frozen food on the continent.** You will only find these products in shops aimed at Western clients, firstly because they are very expensive and secondly because they go against our traditions. Cooking without using fresh produce is unthinkable. This means that vegetables, meat, and fish are rarely bought at supermarkets. Culturally, we buy our food at the market, from our aunt or the woman who calls us "my daughter," "my dear," or "Asso"—a local connection with shopkeepers that you will never find in a supermarket.

- We do not eat like "white people." This may sound pejorative, but should not be taken that way. "Eating like a white person" is quite simply leaving food on the bones. **In Africa, everything that is edible must be eaten.** The same goes for fish—we eat it whole, with the skin, bones, and head.

- **We do not eat baby animals.** Before it is slaughtered, an animal must first have been useful to the community—through its milk if it is a bovine or its eggs if it is a fowl, or by using its muscles to transport goods, etc. Furthermore, given that families are usually large (five children on average), why kill a poor little lamb that's only a year old when a sheep is much plumper and can feed a family of ten people? This is why you will never find recipes with veal or lamb.

- **Food is eaten either raw or well done.** What is meant by "well done" in the West is "very well done" for an African (no traces of blood). The skin of food that is fried or roasted must be well browned or golden.

- Africa is a highly lactose-intolerant region, which is why milk, widely consumed in the West, is not traditionally part of the African diet. Except for some nomadic people groups such as the Peulhs or the Massais, who have raised bovines for thousands of years, **cow, zebu, camel, or goat milk is seldom consumed.** Globalization, however, has meant that several industrial brands have been able to introduce milk in a modified form into African eating habits. This means that you will find various brands of powdered milk as well as evaporated and condensed milk in Africa.

BENEFITS OF
AFRICAN CUISINES

In 2016, West African cuisine was ranked by the World Health Organization as number four in the **top five healthiest cuisines in the world!** That's somewhat surprising for a continent with a cuisine plagued by stereotypes—too oily, too rich, too spicy, too much this, too much that.

According to one study, **traditional West African dishes are considered to be just as healthy as Japanese dishes.** They do actually contain a large number of foods recognized as having health benefits, such as fruit and vegetables, whole grains, dried or smoked fish, or other foods rich in fiber and omega-3.

One of the advantages of African food is also linked to the fact that there are **fewer processed foods on the continent compared to Western countries, and people still only eat the produce that is in season.** This means, for example, that you won't find mangoes if it isn't mango season, and this doesn't surprise anyone—it is considered normal.

Furthermore, in the villages, meals are also a means of healing. Hippocrates said: "Let food be thy medicine, and let medicine be thy food." To observe this in action, it is best to go to rural areas, far from the hustle and bustle of the cities and the pollution that has come with modernization.

MAIN SPECIALTIES

There is an African diet (a food base that's common to all African countries) and then there are African diets, which differ depending on the country, ethnicity, specific food cultures, and geographical resources.

Some of the most common dishes that you will find in most countries include:

• **peanut sauce** in a meat or fish stew, most commonly known as "mafé" in Senegal, "tiguadégué" in Mali, "azindessi" in Togo, and "nfoug owono" in Gabon;

• **cassava leaf stew,** called "saka saka" or "pondu" in the Congo Basin, "ravitoto" in Madagascar, "matapa" in Mozambique, "mataba" in Comoros, "etodjey" in Senegal, or "sauce feuilles" in other West African countries;

• **red palm oil sauce** in a meat or fish stew, called "sauce graine" in the Ivory Coast, "nyembwè" in Gabon, "moambe" in the Congo Basin, and "dekou dessi" in Togo;

• **"pepper soup" or "pèpè soupe,"** which is simply a meat-based stock or one made with offal and/or fish and crustaceans;

• **oily rice,** originally from Senegal, and called "wolof rice" or "jollof rice," can also be found in several West African countries such as Ghana and Nigeria. It becomes "thiep bou dien" when served with vegetables and fish, and "thiep bou yapp" when served with vegetables and meat. In Kenya, this dish is called "riz pilau" and is cooked with meat and Indian spices;

• **okra sauce,** called "supu kandj" (or "soupou kandja") in Senegal, "lalo" in Mauritius, "okra soup" in Ghana and Nigeria, and "fetri dessi" in Togo, is also eaten everywhere in eastern, central, and western Africa;

• **meat and fish are selected** according to availability and religion. In coastal areas, a lot of fresh, dried, and smoked fish is eaten, along with shellfish and crustaceans. Inland, poultry and bovine meat are preferred. More meat is consumed in cities than rural areas since it is more expensive. It is not unusual for families to eat vegetarian meals several times a week and to reserve meat dishes for special occasions.

Yam (or white sweet potato)

Cassava

Taro

Plantain bananas

Sweet potato

Okra

African eggplant

Sweet pepper

STAPLE INGREDIENTS

Tomatoes

Avocado

Pomegranate

African pears

Pineapple

Tamarind

Mango

Lime

Habanero chiles

Mild chiles

Coconut

Ginger

Bananas

STAPLE INGREDIENTS REGION BY REGION

. . . .

WEST AFRICA

Rice is the staple grain, closely followed by millet, sorghum, and fonio. Corn (whole or as cornmeal) and wheat (as flour) are also widely used. In the Sahel region, millet is eaten as a flour or as a semolina, whereas in West Africa, fonio (a type of fine millet) is eaten as a semolina.

The most commonly eaten produce is:

- rice, millet, sorghum, fonio, corn, wheat flour;
- beef, mutton, chicken, guinea fowl, turkey, grouper or white grouper, emperor fish or Nile perch, bass, mullet, crayfish, oysters, shellfish;
- plantain, okra, peanuts, bissap (hibiscus flowers), beet, carrot, turnip, spinach, ginger, root vegetables (yam, cassava, sweet potato, taro, macabo), beans, cashews, African pistachios.

CENTRAL AFRICA

While in West Africa a dish is never eaten without rice, in Central Africa a dish is primarily eaten with a good chunk of cassava tuber, and there are many varieties that exist in all kinds of forms: bobolo, miondo, chikwangue, ogouma, garri ...

The most commonly eaten tubers are cassava, taro, yam, sweet potato, and macabo. Plantains are the next most common food, closely followed by rice and corn.

Given the presence of dense equatorial forests and numerous waterways, game meat, fish, and crustaceans are also regularly enjoyed. Following the various Ebola virus epidemics over the past 20 years, game meat has, however, been gradually replaced by poultry, including chicken, guinea fowl, and turkey. Fish and crustaceans are eaten fresh, salted, dried and/or smoked, seasoned with red palm oil.

The most commonly eaten produce is:

- rice, corn;
- beef, mutton, chicken, guinea fowl, turkey, sea bream, sole, emperor fish or Nile perch, bass, mullet, tilapia, crab, crayfish, oysters, shellfish, lobster;
- cassava, taro, yam, sweet potato, macabo, plantain, beans, peanuts, African pistachios, okra, Guinea sorrel.

EAST AFRICA

The regions of East Africa have been influenced by many different cultures, and as a result they are characterized by many diverse ingredients, flavors, and cooking methods. Dishes are almost always cooked using a large range of spices, which must be of high quality to ensure authentic flavor. The use of freshly ground black peppercorns or 20-year-old cinnamon bark, for example, is key to giving dishes from this region their authentic intensity.

In general, East African cooking usually focuses on grains, slow-cooked stews, curries, and dairy products, which are (especially in the Horn of Africa) infused with a variety of spices and spice mixes of Arab influence (Yemen, Oman, and Egypt) in the north, as well as the Indian connection to the east.

Ethiopian cuisine is undoubtedly the most well-known in East Africa. The country's signature dish is injera, a fermented flatbread made from teff flour, that is springy, slightly sour, and used like a utensil to pick up other food instead of using silverware (a bit like chapati or other Indian flatbreads). The most popular dish served with injera is wat, a thick beef, vegetable, or lentil stew.

The most commonly eaten produce is:

- rice, corn, cassava, sorghum, millet;
- beef, mutton, chicken, sea bream, emperor fish or Nile perch, bass, mullet, tilapia, crab, crayfish, shrimp, sardines;
- beans, lentils, kale, tomatoes, coconut, carrot, sweet pepper;
- pepper, cinnamon, cumin, coriander, cardamom, cloves, fenugreek, tea, curry.

SOUTH AFRICA

As a former trading post, this region carries countless traces of the past, whether they be of Portuguese, Malaysian, Dutch, or even Arab or Indian origin. All the South African countries are meat-eating countries. It is therefore impossible (unless you follow a strict vegetarian diet) to leave this part of the continent without experiencing a local barbecue, called a braai. It is common to all the countries in this region and is a real institution among locals.

The most commonly eaten produce is:

- millet, corn, beans, wheat;
- beef, kudu, springbok, lamb, impala, biltong (dried meat), sausages (boerewors), crab, shrimp, lobster, oysters, fish;
- avocado, cashews, coconut, marula, ginger, lemon, orange, pomelo, grapes, sweet pepper, tomato, cucumber.

Peanut butter

Bissap (hibiscus flowers)

Black-eyed peas

Dried smoked shrimp

African pistachios

Country onions (rondelles)

Cashew nuts

Kinkeliba leaves

Garlic

Onions

Turmeric

Pepper

Soumbala

Garri (fermented, dried, and ground cassava)

THE IDEAL PANTRY

Placali (fermented cassava paste)

Cassava flour

Attiéké (cassava semolina)

Fine cornmeal

Parboiled long-grain rice

Bobolo/ chikwangue/ miondo (cassava bread)

Unrefined red palm oil

Coconut oil

THE IDEAL PANTRY

Have you ever set foot in an African market or grocery store? The mixture of smells, colors, and products makes it a real experience! If you're a beginner, it can be hard to find your way around.

Starchy foods are the major food group represented. The main reason for this is that they are inexpensive, quickly satiating, and come in many forms: fresh, dried, flour, semolina, and couscous. They are a sure bet for people on a tight budget and you should always have some on hand.

After carbohydrates come **vegetables.** There are many varieties of leaves commonly known as "spinach" but they are nothing like spinach as we know it in the West. There are ndolé, sweet potato, taro, cassava, Guinea sorrel, amaranth, okra, and baobab leaves. Other vegetables such as okra, tomatoes, carrots, cabbage, eggplant, and turnips are also popular.

The presence of fruit depends on the region, but it is generally eaten fresh and whole or cut into pieces, or in a fruit salad.

Common cooking aids are spices and oilseeds. A mortar and pestle are essential for working with these. Many people say that African cuisines are very spicy. It's best not to use one country as a generalization, however, as not all African cooking uses spices (e.g. the cuisine of the Maasai people) and is not always spicy (e.g. the cuisine of the nomads in Mauritania). Whereas in West Africa you will find chile in all the sauces, in Central Africa you will find it on the table as a condiment to be added, just like mustard, salt, or pepper.

Marinades rich in spices and aromatics are used to add flavor, and certain mollusks and pungent dried or smoked crustaceans are used to enhance sauces.

Common cooking techniques include grilling over coal or wood, frying, poaching for stocks and soups, smothering, steaming when using leaves to make parcels, slow cooking for sauces, and bain-maries for some terrines or traditional breads made with fermented tubers.

To help you find your way around more easily, here is a (non-exhaustive) list of African pantry essentials. See page 207 for tips on where to source many of these ingredients.

STARCHES AND DERIVATIVES

STARCHES AND GRAINS
- Black-eyed peas
- Corn
- Fonio
- Fufu (cassava starch)
- Millet
- Parboiled long-grain rice
- Sorghum

TUBERS
- Cassava
- Sweet potato
- Taro
- Yam (or white sweet potato)

SEMOLINAS
- Coucous (attiéké for cassava, thiakry for medium millet semolina, araw for rolled millet flour)
- Garri (fermented, dried, and ground cassava)
- Tapioca
- Thiéré (fine millet semolina)

FLOURS
- Cassava flour
- Cornmeal

BREADS
- Bobolo, chikwangue, miondo (all cassava based)

PASTE
- Placali (fermented cassava paste)

FRUIT AND VEGETABLES

FRUIT
- African pear
- Avocado
- Banana
- Baobab fruit
- Coconut
- Guava
- Lemon
- Lime
- Mango
- Papaya
- Passionfruit
- Pineapple
- Pomegranate
- Rockmelon
- Saba senegalensis
- Soursop (custard apple)
- Star fruit
- Strawberry
- Tamarind
- Watermelon

VEGETABLES
- African eggplant
- Cabbage
- Carrot
- Okra
- Plantain
- Sweet pepper
- Tomato
- Turnip

NUTS, SPICES, AND OILSEEDS
- African pistachios
- Baobab seeds
- Cashews
- Country onions (rondelles)
- Djansang (akpi)
- Ginger
- Grains of paradise
- Odika (wild mango seed)
- Peanuts and peanut butter
- Pèbè (Gabon nutmeg)
- Penja pepper, black pepper
- Prekese (tetrapleura tetraptera)
- Soumbala, ground or paste
- Turmeric, fresh or ground

AROMATICS, CONDIMENTS, AND HERBS
- Amaranth, baobab, cassava, Guinea sorrel, kinkeliba, mustard, ndolé, okra, sweet potato, and taro leaves
- Bay leaves
- Bissap (hibiscus flowers)
- Garlic
- Ginger
- Onion
- Parsley
- Small dried shrimp or fish (whole or ground)
- Sweet/mild or habanero chiles (fresh or ground)
- Tamarind
- Thyme
- Tomato paste (concentrated purée)

OILS
- Coconut oil (delicious when used for cooking rice!)
- Neutral vegetable oil (peanut, canola, corn, sunflower)
- Red palm oil (unrefined—rich in vitamin A)

UTENSILS
- Large mortar and fufu (cassava) pestle
- Small mortar and spice pestle
- Wooden spoon

BASES AND APPETIZERS

GREEN NOKOSS

(for fish and crustaceans)

DIFFICULTY: EASY
PREPARATION: 10 MINUTES
COOKING: NONE

INGREDIENTS

1 green sweet pepper

2 mild/sweet green chiles

1 white onion

3 garlic cloves

¾ oz (20 g) fresh ginger

1 celery stalk

2 sprigs thyme

2 sprigs flat-leaf parsley

1 tbsp dried and ground shrimp/fish

PREPARATION

Deseed the sweet pepper and chiles. Peel and roughly chop the onion, garlic, and ginger. Roughly chop the celery.

Using a blender, blend the sweet pepper, chiles, onion, garlic, ginger, celery, and herbs into a smooth paste. Add the dried shrimp and 3 tbsp water, then blend again.

Keep the paste in a glass jar in the fridge.

RED NOKOSS

(for meat)

DIFFICULTY: EASY
PREPARATION: 10 MINUTES
COOKING: NONE

INGREDIENTS

1 red sweet pepper

2 mild/sweet red chiles

1 red onion

3 garlic cloves

¾ oz (20 g) fresh ginger

1 tomato

1 celery stalk

2 sprigs thyme

2 sprigs flat-leaf parsley

1 tbsp soumbala powder (see tip)

PREPARATION

Deseed the sweet pepper and chiles. Peel and roughly chop the onion, garlic, and ginger. Roughly chop the tomato and celery.

Using a blender, blend the sweet pepper, chiles, onion, garlic, ginger, tomato, celery, and herbs into a smooth paste. Add the soumbala and 3 tbsp water, then blend again.

Keep the paste in a glass jar in the fridge.

CHEF ANTO'S TIP

Soumbala is a traditional condiment used in West African cooking and is an ingredient that is widely used, in the same way that fish sauce is used in South-East Asia. It is made by processing the seeds from the pods of the néré tree. It can be found with different names: "nététou" in Senegal, "moutarde africaine" in Togo, "soumbala" in Guinea and Mali, "soumara" in Ivory Coast, and "dadawa" or "iru" in Nigeria and Ghana.

ORANGE NOKOSS

(for vegetables)

DIFFICULTY: EASY
PREPARATION: 20 MINUTES
COOKING: 10 MINUTES

INGREDIENTS

1 carrot	1 leek, white part only
1 yellow onion	1 celery stalk
3 garlic cloves	2 sprigs thyme
¾ oz (20 g) fresh ginger	2 tbsp turmeric
2 mild/sweet chiles	1 tbsp dried smoked fish

PREPARATION

Peel the carrot, onion, garlic, and ginger. Deseed the chiles.

Place the carrot in a pot of salted water and bring to a boil. Cook for 10 minutes, then remove from the water. Roughly chop the carrot, onion, leek, celery, garlic, ginger, chiles, and thyme and combine in a blender.

Blend everything into a smooth paste. Add the turmeric, smoked fish, and 3 tbsp water, then blend again.

Keep the paste in a glass jar in the fridge.

CHEF ANTO'S TIP

Nokoss is a paste used to season sauces, meats, and fish. It will keep longer if you add a layer of vegetable oil to the jar. Store it in the fridge for up to a week. To keep the paste for longer, use an ice-cube tray (that you use for nokoss only) and freeze the whole batch.

NTOROLO

(chile and herb paste)

DIFFICULTY: EASY
PREPARATION: 10 MINUTES
COOKING: NONE

INGREDIENTS

1¾ oz (50 g) hot chiles	⅓ cup (90 ml) vegetable oil
1 white onion	1 tsp salt
5 garlic cloves	
¾ oz (20 g) fresh ginger	

PREPARATION

Cut the tops off the chiles, then roughly chop.

Peel and roughly chop the onion, garlic, and ginger. Combine in a blender with the chile.

Blend everything into a smooth paste, add the oil and salt, then blend again.

Keep the paste in a glass jar in the fridge.

CHEF ANTO'S TIP

Ntorolo is a condiment that is used in the same way as mustard or mayonnaise. Place it on the table to delight guests who love spicy food. If you find it hard to eat really spicy chile, choose mild or sweet chiles, or add red wine vinegar to your jar and the mixture will pack less of a punch.

Orange nokoss

Red nokoss

Green nokoss

Ntorolo

INSTANT MARINADE

DIFFICULTY: EASY · PREPARATION: 15 MINUTES · COOKING: 10 MINUTES

INGREDIENTS

1 bunch flat-leaf parsley

1 bunch cilantro

3 limes

2 tbsp djansang (see tip)

1 tsp Penja pepper

4 tbsp red nokoss
(see p. 26)

Scant 1 cup (200 ml) oil
(peanut, canola, corn,
or sunflower)

PREPARATION

Pick the parsley and cilantro leaves and discard the stems.

Zest and juice the limes.

Toast the djansang and Penja pepper in a dry frying pan over high heat for around 10 minutes. Pound them in a spice mortar.

Combine the nokoss with the lime juice, herbs, ground djansang, and pepper. Mix well. Add the oil and mix again.

Pour the marinade into a jar with the lime zest. Keep refrigerated.

CHEF ANTO'S TIP

Also called "musodo," "erimado," 'corkwood," "akpi," and "essessang," djansang is a fast-growing tree found in western and central Africa. Its nuts are used to add flavor and as a thickener. The djansang kernels are yellow to dark orange in color, depending on the variety, and look very much like chickpeas. If you can't find them, you could substitute ground nutmeg.

NITER KIBBEH

(spiced butter)

DIFFICULTY: EASY · PREPARATION: 20 MINUTES · COOKING: 30 MINUTES

INGREDIENTS

1 French shallot

6 garlic cloves

¾ inch (2 cm) piece fresh ginger

1 cup (250 g) butter

6 basil leaves

A few fragrant verbena leaves

6 cloves

1 tbsp fenugreek

1 tsp saffron or turmeric

1 tsp ground cumin

1 tsp ground nutmeg

½ tsp ground cardamom

½ tsp ground cinnamon

¼ tsp nigella seeds

PREPARATION

Peel the shallot, garlic, and ginger. Finely chop the shallot, crush the garlic, and chop the ginger.

Melt the butter in a saucepan over low heat. Remove from the heat and clarify it by using a small skimmer to remove the froth and whey.

While the butter is still hot, add the shallot, garlic, ginger, and all of the herbs and spices.

Return to the heat and leave to infuse over low heat for 20 minutes.

Remove from the heat, pour the mixture through a fine sieve, then allow it to cool slightly.

Pour the niter kibbeh into an opaque glass jar. Keep refrigerated.

CHEF ANTO'S TIP

Niter kibbeh keeps well for at least a month in the fridge and can even be kept in the freezer for up to a year. It is used in small amounts—1 or 2 spoonfuls per dish—in all kinds of sauces, and especially in Ethiopian recipes, such as kitfo (Ethiopian beef tartare). Using an opaque jar that blocks the light will help preserve its freshness.

STUFFED YAM BALLS

DIFFICULTY: EASY • PREPARATION : 40 MINUTES • COOKING: 30 MINUTES

INGREDIENTS
FOR 6 PEOPLE

1 large yam (or white sweet potato), around 4 lb 8 oz (2 kg)

1 bunch chives

2 tsp turmeric

4 egg yolks

Salt and pepper

14 oz (400 g) ground beef

2 tbsp red nokoss (see p. 26)

Vegetable oil for deep-frying

2 whole eggs

⅔ cup (100 g) garri (fermented, dried, and ground cassava)

PREPARATION

Peel and chop the yam into large pieces. Finely chop the chives.

Cook the yam pieces in a large pot of salted boiling water for 30 minutes. Use a knife to check if the yam is cooked—you should be able to pierce the pieces easily. Drain the yam and then mash while it is still hot.

Add the turmeric, egg yolks, and chives to the mashed yam, season with salt and pepper, and mix well.

In a mixing bowl, combine the beef and red nokoss and season with salt and pepper.

Shape the yam mixture into patties. Place some of the beef filling in the center of each patty and shape the yam around the filling to form a ball.

In a large pot, heat enough oil for deep-frying.

Bread the yam balls by dipping them first into the beaten whole eggs, then in the garri. Fry the yam balls until golden. Drain on paper towels and enjoy.

CHEF ANTO'S TIP

Accompany these yam balls with a spicy tomato sauce as an appetizer or warm snack. If you don't have any garri, regular dried breadcrumbs will be fine.

PAPAYA GAZPACHO

DIFFICULTY: EASY · PREPARATION: 20 MINUTES + OVERNIGHT MARINATING · COOKING: NONE

INGREDIENTS
FOR 4 PEOPLE

1 semi-ripe papaya
(firm flesh)

1 cucumber

½ bunch basil

7 oz (200 g) sliced bread

Scant ½ cup (100 ml) olive oil,
plus extra for drizzling

Scant ½ cup (100 ml) red
wine vinegar

2 tbsp red nokoss (see p. 26)

½ small stale baguette,
cut into pieces, plus extra
to serve

Salt

A few mustard greens

3 tbsp roasted cashews

PREPARATION

Cut the papaya in half and remove the seeds. Peel the papaya and cucumber, then dice the flesh. Chop the basil and the sliced bread.

Combine the papaya, cucumber, basil, and chopped bread in a large bowl. Add the olive oil, red wine vinegar, red nokoss, baguette, and a pinch of salt. Mix and leave to marinate for 24 hours.

Keep a few pieces of papaya aside for garnishing, then purée the papaya mixture until smooth. For an extra-smooth consistency, you can strain the mixture through a sieve. Taste and adjust the seasoning, then place it in the fridge.

To serve, stir the gazpacho and pour it into bowls. Garnish with the reserved papaya pieces, mustard greens, coarsely chopped cashews, and a drizzle of olive oil.

Serve chilled, with thin slices of toasted baguette.

CREAM OF TARO SOUP WITH COCONUT SWIRL

DIFFICULTY: EASY · PREPARATION: 25 MINUTES · COOKING: 25 MINUTES

INGREDIENTS
FOR 6 PEOPLE

7 oz (200 g) taro

¼ red cabbage

2 tbsp green nokoss
(see p. 26)

2 tbsp coconut oil

Salt and pepper

1 bouquet garni (a tied bundle
of herbs such as parsley, bay
leaves, and thyme)

1⅔ cups (400 ml) coconut
cream

A few mustard greens

PREPARATION

Peel the taro, then chop the taro and cabbage into large cubes.

In a large pot, brown the green nokoss in the coconut oil for 5 minutes. Add the taro and cabbage pieces. Season with salt and pepper. Add the bouquet garni and cover with cold water. Leave to cook over medium heat for 20 minutes.

Drain the cooked vegetables, reserving the cooking water, and remove the bouquet garni.

Using a stick blender, finely purée the vegetables, gradually adding the cooking water until smooth and creamy. Adjust seasoning if required.

Whip the coconut cream using a mixer or whipped cream maker.

To serve, divide the warm soup among bowls and spoon the whipped coconut cream on top. Decorate with mustard greens.

CHEF ANTO'S TIP
This soup can be enjoyed either hot or chilled.

CASSAVA AND SHRIMP FRITTERS

DIFFICULTY: EASY · PREPARATION: 45 MINUTES · COOKING: 20 MINUTES

INGREDIENTS
FOR 6 PEOPLE
(AROUND 30 FRITTERS)

3 large cassava tubers,
about 3 lb 5 oz (1.5 kg)

½ bunch herbs—
flat-leaf parsley, chervil,
and/or cilantro

7 oz (200 g) cooked shrimp,
peeled

3 eggs

2 tbsp red nokoss (see p. 26)

Salt and pepper

2 cups (500 ml) oil, for frying

Lime wedges, to serve

PREPARATION

Peel the cassava. Remove the wooden stem in the middle, then grate with a fine grater to get thin strands of cassava.

Place the grated cassava pulp in a clean tea towel and press firmly to remove the liquid.

Finely chop the herbs.

Clean the shrimp, then chop into small pieces.

In a bowl, mix the cassava pulp, eggs, shrimp, herbs, and red nokoss. Season with salt and pepper and mix well. Form the mixture into small fritters, about ½ inch (1 cm) thick.

Heat the oil in a large pot and fry the fritters in batches until golden. Drain on paper towels as you cook them.

Serve the fritters hot as an appetizer or tapas, accompanied by lime weges, thinly sliced crudités, and mashed, seasoned avocado, if you like.

CHEF ANTO'S TIP

Cassava cannot be peeled with a peeler, but needs to be carefully peeled with a knife to properly remove the skin, which is poisonous if ingested. After peeling the cassava, you also need to remove the wooden stem in the middle as it is inedible.

When frying, the oil must not be too hot, otherwise the outside of the fritters will be cooked but not the inside. Check after the first batch to make sure the inside is cooked properly.

If you are allergic to seafood, you can make these as plain fritters without the shrimp or replace the shrimp with leftover roast meat or smoked fish.

Souleymane Coulibaly, or Soro Solo as he is better known, is a radio host born in Korhogo in the Ivory Coast. His informative approach and the 15 or so hours spent weekly on the radio over many years have made him one of the most popular radio hosts in the Ivory Coast. Until the rebellion that broke out in 2002, Soro Solo was one of the most well-known cultural journalists in his country. He is also a two-time recipient of the National Union of Journalists of Ivory Coast award for best journalist in the country (Ebony award, 1993 and 1994).

In 2002, Soro Solo discovered that his name was on the list of people "banned from radio broadcasting until the restructure of services," and some of his family members were assassinated. He was given political asylum in France, where he worked with Radio France Internationale (RFI). He played a key role in introducing African music to Europe and all the biggest African musicians have passed through his studio.

In 2006, Soro Solo produced and co-hosted a daily spot, *L'Afrique enchantée*, with Vladimir Cagnolari, which aired on RFI throughout summer, and then also through winter from 2008 to 2015 (in 2009, *L'Afrique enchantée* was awarded First Prize in francophone radio in the "Magazine" category).

From 2010, Soro Solo once again worked with Vladimir Cagnolari, co-hosting *Le Bal de l'Afrique enchantée*. This program was a raving success across France. In 2015, after Vladimir Cagnolari left the show, Soro Solo renamed it *l'Afrique en Solo* (Africa Solo) and continued to enthusiastically recount the particularities of Africa through special reports and music.

In 2017, Soro Solo was named Knight in the Order of Arts and Letters of the French Republic by the French Ministry for Culture and Communication.

What are your favorite Sub-Saharan African dishes? A star ingredient?

There are many, but I will try and choose just one. One of my favorite dishes is hard to come by and can't be found on restaurant menus. It's a dish from my region, in Sénoufo country, in the savanna in the north of the Ivory Coast. It's a fufu dish with "pistachio" sauce. They're not the same as the pistachios we get here in the West. It's a really flat oilseed (a marrow or squash seed, according to Chef Anto), which we peel, grill, and then crush to obtain a powder to make the sauce. This dish is reserved for famous people and family chiefs, or used to give an extravagant welcome to an important guest.

SORO

The sauce is made with "traditional" ingredients, including onions and fresh tomatoes, which are browned and then left to simmer before being seasoned with pepper and spices and then combined (preferably) with guinea fowl—much tastier than chicken or rooster—that has been browned separately. Once it has all simmered well, we add this "pistachio" powder and leave it to simmer further over low heat. Once the oil from the seeds appears on the surface, it is ready!

The dish can be served with corn-, millet- or sorghum-based dough, but preferably with yam fufu, which is much more sophisticated. The yam tuber is cut into pieces, boiled, and then pounded in a mortar until it turns into a spongy dough.

SOLO

This dough is served in an earthenware dish with the sauce, and you can also add okra or eggplant. Just talking about it is making my mouth water! These days, there are many African dishes that can be found around the world in Washington or Atlanta, Paris or New York. For example, thiep from Senegal or mafé, the peanut-based sauce from Mali. But I have never found the sauce I have just described to you anywhere else!

Does this trigger a taste memory, like Proust's madeleine?
Yes, it does. Speaking about this dish brings back memories from my childhood, of my birthplace, Korhogo, memories of my parents, and also of the village my parents left to move to the city. All of my family are farmers, and my uncles, aunts, and cousins still live in that village today. I spent two months on vacation there every summer.

Sometimes, when a funeral ritual was held to accompany the dead to the afterlife (that's what we believe), the pistachio sauce dish was cooked for important guests and served with yam fufu. Talking about it takes me back to the smells of my village, the smell of the savanna, burnt grass—or incinerated household waste … it brings back all of those smells. It's really something quite specific! It's calming. Even today, after living in France for 16 years, when I return to a country like Burkina Faso or Mali and walk past a house where food is being prepared, I rediscover these smells, as well as the scent of freshly cut vegetables (they are still organic in most of our regions) like okra, chile, or eggplant … Ah, those aromas!

For me, the aroma of the pistachio sauce is just amazing!

What is your connection to this cuisine now?

My job allows me to travel a lot, especially to North and South America as well as Europe. On the other hand, I am not familiar with Asia and have never been there. But wherever I find myself in the world, I have an emotional connection to African cuisine as a whole, and it brings back memories. It reminds me of certain traditions, the things that guide us in life that we are attached to, like a favorite object that gives us a sense of security.

Nowadays, I will sometimes travel all around Paris in search of the Ethiopian dish I tasted in Addis Ababa when I was reporting there, and in doing so will find a cultural connection to my own country. Although Ethiopia isn't my country, there's always a custom or tradition that has a common denominator with my own country or culture. Ethiopian dishes are particular in that they are eaten with your hands, which takes me back to the way of eating at home. I really get the impression that eating with your hands makes the food tastier! That's part of my emotional connection to all African dishes.

Whether it's couscous in Northern Africa, Senegalese thiep, or mafé from Mali, or tô from Burkina Faso, or attiéké from the Ivory Coast, there is an emotional connection, cultural points of reference that allow me to remember what I have been taught on a human, philosophical, and spiritual level. I am a curious person and I enjoy cuisines from around the world. I love French beef bourguignon or a good Italian pizza. But African cooking, with everything familiar that it represents for me, makes me emotional! Sometimes one dish is enough to open up a whole universe. I can find myself daydreaming and forgetting all the worries of the day.

> It reminds me of certain traditions, the things that guide us in life that we are attached to, like a favorite object that gives us a sense of security.

Do you have a tip, a short recipe or any cooking advice?

I don't know how to make tons of dishes, but I can make basic dishes. If I took my time I could make a thiep bou dien, but you really do need to take your time because it is a long and slow dish to make.

I can, however, make dishes that you will find across West Africa (Senegal, Guinea, Mali, Burkina Faso, Ivory Coast, Togo ...), such as mafé (peanut-based sauce), an okra sauce, or even a tomato sauce that's called "clear sauce" in the Ivory Coast because there are no grains used to thicken it. It's made from tomatoes, okra, and eggplant, and I also like to add various different spices that I have discovered in Morocco, Madagascar, or Réunion.

I also know how to make an eggplant sauce that mainly consists of African eggplants, which have a bitter taste. They are crushed to make a paste and, as in all dishes, the onions and crushed tomatoes are browned, then spices and the crushed eggplant are added to make quite a thick and tasty sauce. Meat such as beef or smoked fish can be added as well.

Whatever the dish, it needs to be simmered over low heat for all the ingredients to take on the different flavors. And there is always the same light layer of oil that starts to form on the surface, which means that the dish is cooked! After that, it needs to be simmered for another 10 to 15 minutes to brown and develop a dark orange color and then it will be ready!

To the table ... let's eat!

BASSAMOISE SALAD

INGREDIENTS
FOR 6 PEOPLE

1¼ cups (200 g) dehydrated attiéké (cassava semolina)

⅓ cup (90 ml) olive oil

Salt and pepper

Scant 1 cup (200 ml) boiling water

4 mixed tomatoes (green, black, red, and yellow)

1 cucumber

1 red onion

½ bunch cilantro

½ bunch flat-leaf parsley

½ bunch mint

1 lime

1 lemon

9 oz (250 g) good-quality fresh tuna steak

1 tbsp red wine vinegar

PREPARATION

Pour the cassava semolina into a bowl with 1 tbsp of the olive oil and 1 tsp salt, then mix to coat the semolina with oil. Add the boiling water and mix gently. Cover and leave to rest for 10 minutes, until all the water is absorbed. Fluff using a fork.

Heat the semolina in a dry frying pan over low heat for 5 minutes while continuing to fluff the grains to stop them from sticking together. Leave to cool and set aside.

Cut the tomatoes and cucumber into small cubes. Peel and finely chop the red onion.

Finely chop the herbs and set aside. Zest and juice the lime and lemon.

Cut the tuna into small pieces.

Prepare a dressing using the red wine vinegar, lime and lemon juice, salt, and pepper. Mix well to dissolve the salt. Add the tuna pieces and lime and lemon zest, then leave to marinate for 15 minutes.

To serve, mix the marinated tuna with the tomato and cucumber cubes, herbs, and red onion in a large bowl. Add the remaining olive oil and cooled semolina. Mix gently, adjust the seasoning if required, and serve chilled.

CHEF ANTO'S TIP

Served as a salad or as a side to grilled meat, this bassamoise salad is also suitable for people following a gluten-free diet.

You can find frozen balls of cassava semolina in African grocery stores. If using from frozen, they need to be removed from the freezer the day before. On the day of serving, heat the balls for 2 minutes in the microwave or 10 minutes in a steamer for the semolina to regain its texture.

STUFFED CRABS

DIFFICULTY: MEDIUM · PREPARATION: 1 HOUR · COOKING: 20 MINUTES

INGREDIENTS
FOR 4 PEOPLE

6 x 12 oz (350 g) crabs, or 10½ oz (300 g) crab meat

2 firm tomatoes

¼ cup (50 g) sun-dried tomatoes

2 limes

½ bunch chives

2 tbsp green nokoss (see p. 26)

Vegetable oil

Salt and pepper

4 fresh lasagne sheets (optional)

Turmeric (optional)

FOR SERVING

6 fried okra

2 miondos (thin cassava breadsticks)

1 carrot

A few strands of chives

Lemon zest

PREPARATION

Rinse the crabs, then immerse them in a pot of salted boiling water. Cook for 15 minutes.

When cooked, allow the crabs to cool on a wire rack, then break the pincers, remove the carcasses, and flake the meat. Keep the shells if you plan to use them for serving.

Remove the tomato stems and cut a shallow "X" in the base of each tomato. Immerse the tomatoes in boiling water for 20 seconds to make them easier to peel. Peel, then cut the tomatoes into small cubes. Finely chop the sun-dried tomatoes. Zest and juice the limes. Finely chop the chives.

In a frying pan, sweat the green nokoss with 2 tbsp oil for 3 minutes. Add the crab meat, fresh and sun-dried tomatoes, lime zest, juice, and chives. Reduce for 5 minutes, then season with salt and pepper.

Traditionally, the crab meat is spooned into the shells (hence the name "stuffed crabs"), then cooked in the oven at 350°F (180°C) for 10 minutes. But to be creative, you can use fresh lasagne sheets. Cook the sheets in a pot of salted boiling water with a pinch of turmeric added for 3 minutes each. Immerse the lasagne sheets one at a time, then drain them on paper towels. Leave to cool.

Pipe or spoon the filling onto each lasagne sheet, then roll up the sheet to look like a cannelloni tube. Cut the sheets if they are too big and even up the sides.

Place the rolls in the center of each plate and drizzle with a little oil. Cut the fried okra in half lengthways and place them on the side of the plates. Top the rolls with a few cubes of miondo, some grated and diced carrot, a few chive strands, some grated lemon zest, and a crab pincer. Serve hot.

TUNA PIES

DIFFICULTY: MEDIUM · PREPARATION: 1 HOUR + 1 HOUR RESTING TIME · COOKING: 30 MINUTES

INGREDIENTS FOR
6 PEOPLE (AROUND 20 PIES)

FOR THE PASTRY

3 cups (355 g) all-purpose flour, plus extra for dusting

½ tsp salt

1 tsp baking powder

1 egg, beaten

½ cup (125 ml) warm water or milk

3 tbsp vegetable oil

FOR THE FILLING

5½ oz (150 g) fresh tuna steak

2 tbsp green nokoss (see p. 26)

¼ cup (60 ml) vegetable oil

1 tsp tomato paste

Salt and pepper

Vegetable oil for deep-frying

PREPARATION

For the pastry, combine 2¾ cups (325 g) of the flour, the salt, and baking powder in a bowl. Add the beaten egg and warm water or milk then mix. Gradually add the vegetable oil until the dough is smooth and comes away from the side of the bowl. Dust your work surface with flour and form the dough into a ball, adding more flour if the dough is sticky. Cover and leave to rest for around 1 hour at room temperature.

For the filling, cut the tuna into pieces. In a frying pan, sweat the nokoss with the vegetable oil for 2 minutes. Add the tomato paste, then mix in the tuna pieces and cook for 10 minutes or until the liquid has completely evaporated. Leave to cool completely, then flake the tuna with a fork. Season with salt and pepper.

Roll out the dough to ⅛ inch (3 mm) thick on a floured work surface and use a 3 inch (8 cm) cookie cutter or glass (or any size you like) to cut out rounds.

Place around 1 tsp of filling in the center of each pastry round (more if making larger pies), then fold the pastry to form a pie. Crimp the edges of the pies with a fork to prevent them from opening during cooking.

Heat the oil for deep-frying in a large pot and deep-fry the pies in batches. When each side is nicely golden, remove and drain on paper towels.

CHEF ANTO'S TIP

These pies are great as a hot appetizer or snack. They can be eaten plain, or with a salad or spicy tomato sauce. The tuna can be replaced with mackerel, grouper, or Nile perch. You can also use ground beef or leftover roast meat. For vegetarians, a mix of finely diced sautéed seasonal vegetables or sautéed spinach will also work well.

BLACK-EYED PEA FRITTERS

DIFFICULTY: EASY · PREPARATION: 20 MINUTES + OVERNIGHT SOAKING · COOKING: 30 MINUTES

INGREDIENTS FOR 6 PEOPLE (AROUND 20 FRITTERS)

2½ cups (500 g) dried black-eyed peas (see tip)

2 tbsp orange nokoss (see p. 27)

2 tbsp red palm oil

2 eggs

Salt and pepper

Vegetable oil for deep-frying

PREPARATION

Rinse the peas and leave to soak in a plenty of warm water for a minimum of 12 hours, or overnight.

Vigorously rub the peas between your hands to remove the outer layer of skin, then rinse several times until no skin comes to the surface. Purée the peas in a blender, then gradually add 3½ tbsp water and blend until very smooth, with no lumps. Add the orange nokoss, red palm oil, and eggs and blend. Season with salt and pepper, then blend again.

Insert a star tip onto a pastry bag, then fill with the batter. Heat the oil for deep-frying in a large pot. Form 4 inch (10 cm) logs of batter over the hot oil, cut the batter using scissors, and cook the fritters for around 3 minutes, until golden. Drain on paper towels. Serve with bissap ketchup.

CHEF ANTO'S TIP

Black-eyed peas are called "koki," "niébé," "dolique à œil noir," or "pois à vache," and are a very common bean variety in Sub-Saharan Africa. They are highly nutritious, making them an ingredient of choice for fighting famine and malnutrition. In this recipe, black-eyed peas can be replaced with red kidney beans or black beans.

BISSAP KETCHUP

DIFFICULTY: EASY · PREPARATION : 20 MINUTES · COOKING: 30 MINUTES

INGREDIENTS FOR 4 PEOPLE

⅓ cup (20 g) dried bissap (hibiscus) flowers / 4 large ripe tomatoes / 3 tbsp sugar / 1 tbsp orange nokoss (see p. 27) / 2 tbsp wild honey / 2 tbsp red wine vinegar / Salt and Penja pepper

PREPARATION

Place the bissap flowers and 1 cup (250 ml) water in a small saucepan. Bring to a boil and cook until the water has reduced by half. Remove the tomato stems, then cut a shallow "X" in the base of each tomato. Immerse them in boiling water for 20 seconds. Peel the tomatoes, remove the seeds, and finely dice. Heat the sugar in a separate pot until a pale caramel forms. Add the tomato and mix well. Cook for 3 minutes, then stir in the orange nokoss and honey. Deglaze the pan with the red wine vinegar and reduced bissap juice. Leave to stew for 15 minutes, stirring regularly. Season with salt and pepper. Blend until the sauce is smooth.

FONIO SALAD WITH MANGO

DIFFICULTY: EASY · PREPARATION: 35 MINUTES · COOKING: 15 MINUTES

INGREDIENTS
FOR 4 PEOPLE

2 ripe mangoes with firm flesh

1 red onion

⅔ cup (100 g) cherry tomatoes

¼ bunch flat-leaf parsley

¼ bunch mint

¼ bunch cilantro

2½ tbsp roasted cashews

2 limes

1 tsp green nokoss (see p. 26)

Salt and pepper

Generous 1 cup (200 g) fonio (see tip)

⅓ cup (90 ml) vegetable oil

PREPARATION

Peel and finely dice the mangoes and onion. Cut the tomatoes in half and finely dice. Finely chop the herbs. Roughly crush the cashews.

Zest and juice the limes into a large bowl, then mix in the green nokoss. Season with salt and pepper.

Rinse the fonio several times in clean water. Steam the fonio in a couscoussier or cheesecloth-lined steamer for 15 minutes. Fluff the fonio with a fork, then mix in 1 tbsp of the oil. Leave to cool in a bowl.

Add the remaining oil to the lime and nokoss mixture and whisk vigorously. Add the mangoes, tomatoes, herbs, and onion. Add the fonio, a little at a time, and mix well. Garnish the salad with the crushed cashews.

Serve chilled.

CHEF ANTO'S TIP

Black or white fonio is a gluten-free grain with many benefits. Long considered a foodstuff of the poor, fonio has been grown in West Africa since 5000 BC. It's rich in mineral salts and amino acids and is a great choice for those with gluten intolerance. It's similar to sorghum or rice in its composition and is therefore suitable for people with coeliac disease. Fonio is generally prepared as a couscous or as a mash to accompany all kinds of dishes. You can find it in African grocery stores and healthfood stores.

NGONDO
(African pistachio loaf)

DIFFICULTY: MEDIUM · PREPARATION: 20 MINUTES + 3 HOURS RESTING TIME · COOKING: 1 HOUR

INGREDIENTS
FOR 6 PEOPLE

1 onion

1 mild/sweet green chile

1 lb 2 oz (500 g) African pistachios or pumpkin seeds (see tip)

1 tbsp red nokoss (see p. 26)

3½ oz (100 g) smoked mackerel, flaked

Salt and pepper

6 banana leaves

PREPARATION

Peel and finely chop the onion. Deseed and finely chop the chile.

Use a blender to process the African pistachios to a powder or use a mortar and pestle to crush them until they are reduced to a powder. Set aside in a bowl.

To prepare a stock, pour 1 cup (250 ml) water into a pot with the red nokoss, onion, chile, flaked mackerel, and salt, and bring to a boil. Gradually add the hot stock to the African pistachio powder until a smooth paste forms.

Wash the banana leaves and pass them over a flame until they soften and become pliable. Spread the leaves over the base of a baking dish, pour the paste over the top and fold the leaves over the paste. Place the dish in a couscoussier (see tip) and steam for 45 minutes. Preheat the oven to 350°F (180°C).

Transfer the dish to the oven for 15 minutes to dry the loaf. Leave to cool for 1 hour at room temperature, then for at least 2 hours in the fridge.

Turn out, unwrap, slice, and serve with a cassava bread such as bobolo or kwanga cassava, or with plantain fufu (page 130).

CHEF ANTO'S TIP

African pistachios (pictured on p. 20) are the almond-shaped seeds found in different types of squash, melon, or gourd. These seeds are regularly eaten in Western and Central Africa in the form of a terrine cooked in banana leaves—"ngondo" or pistachio loaf in Cameroon, Congo, and Gabon. If you don't have any banana leaves, use parchment paper or foil. If you don't have a couscoussier, you can use a bain-marie— just ensure that the water reaches halfway up the baking dish. This loaf is eaten cold and mustn't be reheated, or you may end up spending the day in the bathroom!

AFRICAN PEAR DIP AND YAM CHIPS

DIFFICULTY: EASY • PREPARATION : 20 MINUTES • COOKING: 10 MINUTES

INGREDIENTS
FOR 6 PEOPLE

- yam (or white sweet potato), around 2 lb 4 oz (1 kg)
- Vegetable oil for deep-frying
- 2 African pears (see tip)
- lime
- ½ ripe avocado
- tbsp green nokoss (see p. 26)
- 2 tbsp coconut cream
- tsp sugar
- tbsp vegetable oil
- Salt
- A few mustard greens

PREPARATION

Peel and wash the yam and pat dry with paper towel. Cut the yam in half lengthways, then cut each half into very thin slices using a knife or mandolin.

In a large pot, heat oil for deep-frying and deep-fry the chips. Drain on paper towels and set aside in a dry place.

Place the pears in a heatproof bowl.

Bring a pot of water to a boil, then turn off the heat, pour the water over the pears, and cover. Leave to soften for 10 minutes, then drain the pears and let them cool. Carefully remove the thin skin as it is astringent and sometimes bitter. Scoop out the flesh by scraping the fruit with the blade of a knife.

Zest and juice the lime. Peel the avocado.

Combine the pear and avocado flesh, lime juice, green nokoss, coconut cream, sugar, and vegetable oil and blend until very smooth. Season with salt and pepper.

Decorate the dip with the mustard greens and lime zest and serve with the yam chips.

CHEF ANTO'S TIP

African pears (Dacryodes edulis) are sometimes called "atanga," "safou," and "ube." If you can't find them, you could substitute 6–8 small, firm, tart pears. In this recipe, the avocado tempers the very sour flesh of the pears. To make it even creamier, add more coconut cream. This dip will keep for 24 hours in the fridge.

Born in Bamako, Mamani Keïta is an Afro-pop singer from Mali, belonging to the Madinka people group.

She won the Bamako Commune prize for Best Solo Artist at the 1982 Artistic Biennale, then went on to join the Bamako District Orchestra, then the National Badema Orchestra. She caught the attention of Salif Keïta, a famous albino Malian singer, who took her to France in 1987 as a backing vocalist for his concerts. Mamani Keïta then contributed to several of Salif Keïta's albums (*Soro, Ko-Yan, Amen*) and tours. She moved to Paris in 1991; unable to leave France as she didn't hold a residency permit, she continued to perform at her mentor's concerts in mainland France.

The singer participated in various projects combining African music and jazz (Hank Jones and Cheick Tidiane Seck), but it was

In 2015, Mamani Keïta joined her fellow singers in the supergroup Les Amazones d'Afrique. Using their powerful and complementary voices, they rallied together to support the fight for women's empowerment, especially in Africa.

In 2018, the group Arat Kilo, a French group with Ethiopian influence, invited Mamani Keïta and the American rapper Mike Ladd to contribute to their album *Visions of Selam*, which mixes Bambara, Creole, and English to take listeners on a journey across the African continent.

Mamani Keïta is not only one of the biggest voices in Mali, a singer who knows how to capture, seduce, and electrify her audience, she also has imposing charisma and incredible talent for musical open-mindedness, making her an independent and dedicated artist.

MAMANI

with her *Electro Bamako* album in 2002 that she started to make a name for herself and reveal the full extent of her vocal skills. She performed a duet with musician/singer Marc Minelli on this project.

In 2006, Mamani released the album *Yelema* in another collaboration, this time with French guitarist, arranger, and producer Nicolas Repac, and the music is subtly highlighted by his long-time partner Arthur H. Mamani's unique voice and Nicolas Repac's understated samples.

Her electro-rock album *Gagner l'argent français*, released in 2011 and produced by Nicolas Repac, talks about issues such as immigration, the economic crisis, and politics.

www.facebook.com/mamanikeitamusic
www.instagram.com/@mamani.keita

KEÏTA

What are your favorite Sub-Saharan African dishes? A star ingredient?

It would have to be mafé! I am a Mandinka and mafé comes from us, the Keïta clan.

Mafé is made using peanut butter and the sauce is prepared with onions and meat, and is often served with rice. Nowadays, mafé has become the most well-known dish in Sub-Saharan African cuisine; all African restaurants have mafé on their menus—it's something that we Mandinkas can be proud of! That means my favorite ingredient will always be peanuts, but also African eggplant and chile. The blend of chile in mafé makes it really addictive!

Does this trigger a taste memory, like Proust's madeleine?

Yes, and one particular memory really left its mark. One day my maternal grandmother sent me to the market to get some groceries because she was really busy. I was eight years old and that day was the first time I made a dish on my own, without help from my grandmother or my aunt. They had gone to the hospital to get an eye problem looked at and had asked me to get the groceries at the market while they were gone, thinking they would be home in time to prepare the meal. At 8am I went to the market with the list my aunt had given me and returned home around 10am. Time continued to pass and they didn't come back, so I decided to start preparing the meal. At the time, we didn't have the means to use peanut butter, so we used shea butter instead. I mustn't have done everything exactly right, but overall I was pretty proud of myself. I had made mafé!

When they returned, my aunt went to start cooking and asked me if the shopping had been done, but I told her that the meal was ready, that I had already made it. My aunt starting shouting: "Oh my goodness! We are not going to eat today, she's going to kill us!" She went into the kitchen, looked in the pot and asked me: "Did you make this?!"

They were both pleasantly surprised.

Since that day, I have never stopped cooking!

I was raised by my maternal grandmother and aunt (my mother's younger sister), and whenever they were preparing a meal, I watched everything. That's how I learned how to cook.

What is your connection to this cuisine now?

The connection is still very much with me. I still cook African cuisine just as often, even though I have lived in France for a long time now. Sometimes I cook something "Western" with pasta or beans, for example, but more often than not, I cook African food. I have passed on what I know to my daughter, who now cooks African recipes. She has taken up the baton of African cuisine!

Do you have a tip, a short recipe, or any cooking advice?

I recommend learning how to cook African food—there are a lot of resources available.

I do, however, use peanut oil and avoid using palm oil. It doesn't really agree with me and I find it too heavy. Sara sara sauce (spinach sauce with okra) is a lot less oily using peanut oil.

When it comes to mafé, I can make three different versions. One version is plain, made with peanut butter only, another version has spinach leaves as well as peanut butter, and a final version has okra.

> Nowadays, mafé has become the most well-known dish in Sub-Saharan African cuisine; all African restaurants have mafé on their menus.

BLACK-EYED PEA AND BEET HUMMUS

DIFFICULTY: MEDIUM · PREPARATION: 40 MINUTES + OVERNIGHT SOAKING · COOKING: 1 HOUR

INGREDIENTS
FOR 6 PEOPLE

2 cups (400 g) dried black-eyed peas (see tip p. 50)

9 oz (250 g) raw red beets

2 limes

Scant ½ cup (100 ml) olive oil

2 tbsp red nokoss (see p. 26)

2 tbsp cashew butter

Salt and pepper

FOR SERVING

⅓ cup (50 g) roasted cashews

1 scallion

3 sprigs cilantro

PREPARATION

Rinse the peas and leave to soak in plenty of warm water for a minimum of 12 hours, or overnight.

Vigorously rub the peas between your hands to remove the outer layer of skin, then rinse several times until no skin comes to the surface.

Preheat the oven to 400°F (200°C). Wrap the beets in foil, place in the oven, and roast for 1 hour or until tender when pierced with a knife. Remove the beets from the foil, leave to cool, and peel. Cut the beets into small pieces and place in a blender.

Zest and juice the limes. Drain the peas, then add them to the blender with the beets, olive oil, red nokoss, cashew butter, and lime juice. Blend for around 3 minutes until the mixture is very smooth. Mix in the lime zest and season with salt and pepper to taste.

Serve chilled, sprinkled with crushed cashews, thinly sliced scallion, and cilantro leaves.

CHEF ANTO'S TIP

This hummus is delicious with toasted bread rubbed with garlic or a cassava bread such as chikwangue or bobolo, or as a side to grilled dishes, in salads, and even on sandwiches. This recipe will also work with packaged cooked beets. You just need to make sure the beets are well drained since the flesh often contains water and could make the hummus too runny.

KACHUMBARI SALAD

DIFFICULTY: EASY · PREPARATION: 30 MINUTES · COOKING: NONE

INGREDIENTS
FOR 6 PEOPLE

2 small red onions

1 mild/sweet green chile

3 multicolor mini sweet peppers

6 mixed tomatoes (green, black, and red)

20 yellow cherry tomatoes

3 limes

¼ bunch cilantro

¼ bunch chervil

Salt and pepper

⅓ cup (90 ml) vegetable oil

PREPARATION

Peel the onions. Deseed the chile and cut in half lengthways. Use the tip of a small knife to remove the seeds from the sweet peppers, keeping the sweet peppers whole.

Carefully remove the stems from the tomatoes and cut a shallow "X" in the base of each. Immerse the tomatoes in boiling water for 20 seconds to make them easier to peel. Peel the cherry tomatoes and keep them whole. To make tomato petals, peel the green, black and red tomatoes, cut into quarters, remove the flesh, and pat them dry with paper towels.

Finely dice the chile and slice the mini sweet peppers into thin rounds. Cut the red onions in half first, then thinly slice them lengthways.

Zest and juice the limes. Pick the leaves from the herbs and chop finely.

To prepare the dressing, combine the salt, pepper, and lime juice in a bowl. Add the lime zest and oil.

Arrange the tomato petals into a rosette, top with the cherry tomatoes, sliced onions, and mini sweet peppers, and sprinkle with the diced chile. Drizzle with the dressing and scatter the herbs on top.

CHEF ANTO'S TIP
Kachumbari salad is found everywhere in countries such as Kenya, Tanzania, and Malawi. It is served as a side with all dishes. Traditionally made with tomatoes, onions, and chile with a lime juice dressing, you can add whatever ingredients you have on hand, such as avocado, mango, cucumber, and radish.

KITFO
(Ethiopian beef tartare)

DIFFICULTY: EASY · PREPARATION: 30 MINUTES · COOKING: 2 HOURS

INGREDIENTS
FOR 6 PEOPLE

1 lb 5 oz (600 g) beef steak

3 yellow (very ripe) limes

6 scallions

3 sprigs cilantro

3 sprigs flat-leaf parsley

1 fresh chile

2 tbsp red nokoss (see p. 26)

1 tsp mild paprika

Salt and pepper

4 tbsp niter kibbeh (see p. 31)

A few baby spinach leaves

FOR THE GARRI CRACKERS

1 tsp red palm oil

Salt

⅔ cup (100 g) garri
(fermented, dried, and
ground cassava)

PREPARATION

To prepare the garri crackers, bring 1 cup (250 ml) water to a boil with the red palm oil and a pinch of salt, pour in the garri, and mix vigorously until it forms a dough that comes away from the side of the pot. Gather the dough into a ball.

While the dough is still hot, place the ball between two sheets of parchment paper and use a rolling pin to flatten it to $\frac{1}{16}$ inch (1 mm) thick. (The dough must be very thin so that the crackers dry quickly.) Cut out rounds from the dough with a cookie cutter and dry them in the oven for 2 hours at 200°F (100°C).

Use a knife to cut the beef into small cubes.

Zest and juice the limes and finely chop the scallions and herbs. Deseed and finely dice the chile. Mix the chopped beef in a bowl with the red nokoss, lime zest, scallions, herbs, chile, and paprika. Season with salt and pepper.

To make the dressing, mix the niter kibbeh with the lime juice, then stir it through the beef mixture.

Serve the beef tartare well chilled, accompanied by the baby spinach and garri crackers.

CHEF ANTO'S TIP

Garri is fermented and dried cassava semolina, which can be prepared as a sweet or savory dish.

Kitfo, or ketfo, is an Ethiopian and Eritrean dish of finely minced raw beef mixed with a spice powder called mitmita, and a spiced butter called niter kibbeh. Kifto is often served on injera, a teff flour crepe, and served with fromage frais and green vegetables. The meat is marinated in lime juice and spices. If you're not a fan of marinated raw meat, you can pan-fry your tartare for a few minutes.

SEA BASS CARPACCIO WITH GREEN MANGO

DIFFICULTY: EASY · PREPARATION: 45 MINUTES · COOKING: NONE

INGREDIENTS
FOR 6 PEOPLE

3 whole sea bass, or
6 x 5½ oz (150 g) sea bass fillets

2 tbsp vegetable oil

2 green mangoes

½ red onion

1 lime

¼ pomegranate

3 sprigs cilantro

Salt and Penja pepper

3 tbsp mango purée

1 tsp ntorolo (see p. 27)

A few croutons

A few baby spinach leaves

PREPARATION

Wash the bass fillets and remove the skin and bones. Brush them with the oil, then lay them flat in a container before putting them in the freezer for 30 minutes to firm up.

To prepare the mango relish, peel and finely dice the green mangoes and red onion. Zest and juice the lime. Remove the seeds from the pomegranate. Finely chop the cilantro.

In a bowl, mix the diced green mangoes, red onion, lime zest, pomegranate seeds, and chopped cilantro. Season with salt and pepper.

Make a dressing with the lime juice, mango purée, and ntorolo and season with salt and pepper. Mix the dressing with the mango relish.

Remove the fish from the freezer, cut it into very thin slices, and arrange on a serving plate. Serve immediately with the mango relish, small croutons, baby spinach leaves, and a few Penja peppercorns.

CHEF ANTO'S TIP

Green mangoes are part of my childhood memories. Children, impatiently waiting for the mangoes to ripen, pick the green ones to eat with salt and chile. This relish is a perfect accompaniment to raw fish, ceviche, or even salads. Sea bass can be replaced with shrimp, sea bream, emperor fish, Nile perch, or barramundi.

MAINS

STUFFED MULLET

DIFFICULTY: MEDIUM • PREPARATION: 45 MINUTES • COOKING: 30 MINUTES

INGREDIENTS
FOR 4 PEOPLE

1 large mullet, around
3 lb 5 oz (1.5 kg)

1½ tbsp (20 g) butter

½ bunch flat-leaf parsley

1 bay leaf

1 French shallot

Salt and pepper

1¾ oz (50 g) stale sliced
bread

3½ tbsp milk

4 tomatoes

2 tbsp chopped cilantro

3 tbsp green nokoss
(see p. 26)

Olive oil

Thyme sprigs

2 mild/sweet green
chiles (optional)

PREPARATION

Remove the scales, fins, and gills from the fish and gut it through the head. Using a very sharp knife, split the skin along the backbone and carefully remove the bone without piercing the skin. Remove the meat from the bones and place it in the fridge. Keep the fish head and skin intact and place them in the fridge. Reserve the fish bones and fins.

To prepare the fish stock, melt the butter in a pot with the roughly chopped parsley stems, bay leaf, and chopped shallot. Sweat for 2 minutes. Add the fish bones, fins, and 1¼ cups (300 ml) water and bring to a boil. Strain, then season with salt and pepper.

To prepare the stuffing, soak the stale bread in the milk. Peel three of the tomatoes, remove the seeds, and cut the flesh into small cubes. In a blender, finely chop the cilantro and parsley leaves. Add the fish meat, green nokoss, and tomato cubes. Squeeze the bread to remove the excess liquid, then add the bread to the fish mixture and season with salt and pepper.

Preheat the oven to 300°F (150°C).

To stuff the fish, take the fish skin with the head and fill it with stuffing so that it regains its original shape. Be careful not to overfill it or it may burst during cooking. Using a large needle and kitchen twine, sew up the skin along the back opening.

Drizzle some olive oil in a roasting pan and sprinkle it with thyme and salt. Place the stuffed mullet on top and add the whole chiles (if using) beside the fish. Drizzle the fish with olive oil and cover with foil. Bake for 10 minutes, then remove the foil, pour the fish stock over the top, and cook for a further 20 minutes.

Slice the remaining tomato and arrange it on top of the fish to serve.

CHEF ANTO'S TIP

The stuffing tastes better if it's prepared a day ahead. If there's any stuffing left over once the fish is sewn up, insert it gently through the head, without overfilling. The mullet can be replaced with sea bass or another firm-fleshed fish.

FAT RICE

DIFFICULTY: MEDIUM · PREPARATION: 45 MINUTES · COOKING: 2 HOURS

INGREDIENTS
FOR 4 PEOPLE

1 guineafowl or small chicken, about 2 lb 4 oz (1 kg)

⅔ cup (150 ml) vegetable oil

3 tbsp red nokoss (see p. 26)

4 tsp soumbala (see tip p. 26)

Salt and pepper

2 cups (400 g) long-grain rice

2 large onions

½ bunch flat-leaf parsley, plus sprigs, to serve

2 tomatoes

1 mild yellow chile, plus extra to serve

Lemon wedges, to serve

PREPARATION

Wash the guineafowl, cut it into pieces, and rinse.

Heat a third of the oil in a large heavy-based pot and brown the guineafowl pieces. Add half the nokoss and half the soumbala and sweat, then cover with water and season with salt and pepper. Cook over low heat until the meat is tender, about 45 minutes.

Bring some water to a boil in a couscoussier (or a steamer lined with cheesecloth) to partially cook the rice. Wash the rice and set it above the couscoussier. Cover and cook the rice for 10 minutes. Stir, then cook for a further 10 minutes. The rice is ready when the surface of the rice is hard (difficult to poke a finger through). Remove the rice from the heat, then cover and set aside.

Peel and slice the onions, pick the parsley leaves, and dice the tomatoes. Heat the remaining oil in a large Dutch oven or heavy pot and sweat half the onion over medium heat. Blend the remaining onions with the parsley leaves, tomato, 1 tsp pepper, and the remaining soumbala and nokoss to make a paste. Gently mix this paste into the cooking onion and cook over low heat until it becomes golden and caramelized.

Transfer the meat to the caramelized onion mix, reserving the cooking liquid, add the whole chile, and simmer for 10 minutes. Remove the meat and chile and set aside.

Stir the rice into the caramelized onions. Add the liquid from cooking the meat and enough water so that the rice is covered by ½ inch (1 cm). Cover and cook over low heat for 15 minutes.

Stir the rice, place the meat pieces on top, then cover and cook for a further 15 minutes.

Serve the meat and rice with parsley sprigs, whole chiles, and lemon wedges.

DG CHICKEN

DIFFICULTY: EASY • PREPARATION: 1 HOUR • COOKING: 45 MINUTES

INGREDIENTS
FOR 4 PEOPLE

3 lb 5 oz (1.5 kg) free-range chicken

3 large carrots

1 green sweet pepper

1 red sweet pepper

1 leek, white part only

3 tbsp curry powder

Vegetable oil

2 cups (500 ml) chicken stock

Salt and pepper

2 semi-ripe plantains

FOR THE MARINADE

1 white onion

2½ oz (70 g) fresh ginger

3 garlic cloves

½ bunch flat-leaf parsley

1 lime

1 tbsp djansang (see tip p. 30)

1 tsp pèbè (see tip p. 80)

1 mild/sweet chile

Vegetable oil

PREPARATION

Rinse the chicken and pat dry, then cut it into pieces.

To make the marinade, peel and quarter the onion, ginger, and garlic. Pick the parsley leaves and juice the lime. Dry roast the djansang and pèbè over low heat for 10 minutes. Put the parsley leaves, onion, ginger, garlic, lime juice, roasted spices, and chile in a blender. Blend, adding oil a little at a time, until the marinade is smooth but not too runny.

Preheat the oven to 350°F (180°C). Mix the chicken pieces with two-thirds of the marinade on a baking tray. Bake for 30 minutes.

Peel the carrots and cut them into thick rounds. Deseed and thinly slice the sweet peppers. Slice the leek into thin sticks. In a large Dutch oven or heavy pot, heat a little oil and sweat the carrots, sweet peppers, and leek with the curry powder until they are slightly browned.

Add the remaining marinade and chicken stock, season with salt and pepper, and cook over medium heat for 15 minutes.

Peel the plantains and use the back of a knife to gently scrape the flesh to remove the thin bitter layer. Cut the plantains into 1¼ inch (3 cm) rounds and salt lightly.

Heat enough oil for deep-frying in a large pot to 350°F (180°C) and deep-fry the plantain rounds until golden. Remove from the oil and keep warm.

Add the chicken pieces to the pot with the vegetables and simmer for 10 minutes.

Serve the chicken and vegetables topped with the fried plantains.

With a voice that ranges from a whisper to a full-throated cry, performer and actress Sandra Nkaké's world seemingly knows no bounds. The first time you hear the young woman's voice and see her fiery temperament, you will be lost for words.

From the first notes she sings, Sandra Nkaké is a knockout. With her Franco-Cameroonian background, she brings together jazz, soul, and song with unparalleled talent and creativity. Sandra Nkaké is uncompromising, authentic, and generous. Soul diva, crazy rocker, and spoken-word singer, she slams, proclaims, and invents a world that she continues to recreate and explore.

Sandra Nkaké is one of the voices that stands out in the French music scene. After two solo albums (*Mansaadi* and *Nothing for Granted*), a Victoire accolade in 2012 awarded by the French Ministry of Culture to recognize outstanding achievement in the music industry ("Revelation jazz" and winner of the Franck Ténot prize), and several collaborations (Jî Mob, Grand Corps Malade, Autour de Chet),

composing a collection of arty and stripped-back songs with Jî Drû, her long-standing ally, that are like little stories whispered in your ear: *Tangerine Moon Wishes*.

Sandra Nkaké has found her groove in a completely new musical space, one that belongs only to her. Through her majestic voice and collaboration with Jî Drû, a new genre has been born: fanciful, ghostly, reflective, personal, and minimal. An introspective and glowing journey, totally weightless, suspended on Sandra's breath and words.

Sandra Nkaké is a musical UFO. Now it's your turn to encounter this extraordinary artist-author, composer, and performer. She is totally unique.

SANDRA

she has charmed crowds and critics during performances at some of the biggest pop and jazz festivals in France and during an international tour over the past four years. She is an artist blessed with a multi-faceted voice, deep, powerful, and fragile at the same time, and one that takes on an even more incredible quality on stage—a gift appreciated by a growing number of fans. For her third album, released in September 2017, Sandra throws the doors open to her world,

www.sandrankake.com
www.facebook.com/sandrankake
www.instagram.com/sandrankake
www.youtube.com/user/sandrankake

What are your favorite Sub-Saharan African dishes? A star ingredient?

It's difficult to choose, but number one would have to be ndolé, in tribute to the land where I was born, and it's also a dish that I love and that I miss. This dish is deeply connected to my childhood, to my first memories of smells, colors, and spending time with my family.

I love yassa, I love mafé and make it often, and I also love thiep, however it takes a long time to make and I don't do it. It's too hard to choose! But let's say that the top three are ndolé, then mafé, because we make it often and the children ask for it, and finally yassa!

I like the mix of the bitterness of the spinach and the sweetness of the peanuts and onions in ndolé. When I can't use the proper leaves for ndolé because they aren't fresh (they're most commonly found frozen), I try to replace them with organic spinach and it works well.

Does this trigger a taste memory, like Proust's madeleine?

Yes, but it's not a memory directly connected to ndolé as a dish. It's a memory of being with my grandfather. I was partly raised by my grandparents. My grandfather did not often cook, but when he did, he did everything himself, from start to finish. He would go to the market himself, choose the ingredients, and do the shopping. One day he took me with him. We went to the market together, and it took at least two hours, mainly discussing different ingredients with several ladies.

There is another delicious dish that I love, called moukon (moukon ma ngondo)! This is another dish my grandfather would cook, made from palm weevil larvae, and we had to choose the larvae together. It was great, firstly because I got to spend time discovering things with my grandfather, but also because it helped me understand that before any dish gets to your plate, there is a whole series of steps to take, especially the step of selecting the ingredients, which, in the case of the larvae, was live produce! The larvae were white, with a small black head. I was not at all prepared for what I would see and I was a bit shocked. The larvae for my grandfather's pâté needed to be fat (at least they seemed very fat to me!) and the selection process was painstaking. He wanted all of them to be the same size, rather fat, but not too fat. Once his bag was full and we returned home, the next task was to empty the larvae. To do this, you have to split the larvae in half a bit like a snow pea or green bean and all of the white comes out of the larvae—it's quite disgusting! Told like this, it doesn't sound very appetizing, but once it's been cooked with onions, garlic, ginger, and lots of spices, such as djansang (also called akpi seeds—tiny yellowish seeds that you crush with a stone), it really was delicious!

And you know, eating is more than just feeding yourself, it's also sharing, exploring, learning ...

This memory certainly left its mark, but it's more a memory of spending time with my grandfather. And you know, eating is more than nourishment, it's also sharing, exploring, learning ... a wonderful memory! It was in Yaoundé, but the recipe is from his village—Fico, a very small village not far from the city of Douala.

What is your connection to this cuisine now?
I don't cook this type of food much as there are many things that I didn't learn, but on the other hand, I eat it a lot! So, the connection comes through the restaurants I enjoy going to and some foods are always included in my diet, such as chile, ginger, and ndolé, when I get a chance to make it. But what I do cook the most is mafé. Although it's not a dish from Cameroon, in our busy urban life, it's

faster and easier to make than ndolé. I also like yam and cassava a lot and I eat them regularly (it's as if I get a sudden craving for it) and I like okra, too. I like drinking bissap and ginger juice; I'm actually very picky with my ginger juice and I don't like it when it's too sweet. I'm picky with ndolé, too—I don't like it when there's too much peanut. I like to taste the bitterness—it's almost like the raw taste of the earth.

Cooking is also an opportunity to spend time with my children—three out of the four of them know how to make mafé. They love preparing food! We often try recipes together. Sometimes we collapse in a heap of laughter when the result is not what we were expecting. It's really fun when we experiment together. We try to limit sugar, especially refined sugar, and try to limit preservatives and additives too.

We research and we test! It's actually my children who are curious about all this—they like to smell, taste, and ask how to do things. For example, my daughter started to make mafé only when she left home, for her friends. A statement of her African heritage, perhaps.

Do you have a tip, a short recipe, or any cooking advice?
Take your time, leave dishes to simmer, don't try and go too fast! Other than that, I am perhaps a bit of a grandmother when I cook, and I like to line up my ingredients according to each one's cooking time. As a result, I decide whether or not to peel them so as to avoid oxidation.

Even though, in general, I would say that I'm a pretty disorganized person, when it comes to cooking, I do need things to be ordered—for example, I need to follow the recipe, whereas my mother liked to improvise much more, being creative with what was in the fridge.

BEEF KONDRÈ

DIFFICULTY: MEDIUM • PREPARATION: 1 HOUR • COOKING: 4 HOURS

INGREDIENTS
FOR 4 PEOPLE

2 tomatoes

2 onions

3 garlic cloves

1 mild/sweet chile

1 tbsp freshly grated ginger

1 tbsp crushed djansang
(see tip p. 30)

1 tbsp ground prekese
(see tip)

1 tbsp pèbè (see tip)

2 green plantains

2 lb 4 oz (1 kg) beef pieces
(short ribs or chuck steak)

Salt and pepper

2 tbsp palm oil or neutral
vegetable oil

4 cups (1 liter) beef stock

1 bouquet garni (a tied bundle
of herbs such as parsley, bay
leaves, and thyme)

PREPARATION

Peel the tomatoes, onions, and garlic. Dice the tomatoes, thinly slice the onions, crush the garlic, and finely chop the chile. Mix the tomato, onion, garlic, and chile with the ginger and spices. Set aside.

Peel the plantains and use the back of a knife to gently scrape the flesh to remove the thin bitter layer. Cut each plantain into thirds and set aside in a bowl of water.

Season the beef pieces with salt and pepper. Heat half of the oil in a Dutch oven or heavy pot and brown the beef over medium–high heat. Set the browned beef aside.

Tip the plantains into the pot and sprinkle in three-quarters of the tomato mixture. Add the stock and bouquet garni and season with salt and pepper. Cover and cook over low heat for 30 minutes.

Transfer the plantain pieces to a bowl. Add the beef to the pot and stir, then simmer over low heat for 3 hours.

Mix the remaining tomato mixture and remaining oil into the stew. Add the plantains and cook for a further 30 minutes.

Leave the stew to rest for 10 minutes before serving.

CHEF ANTO'S TIP

Kondrè is a recipe originally from Cameroon. It's a beef stew prepared with plantains. Spices such as pèbè, djansang, and prekese (also called tetrapleura tetraptera, "4 sides," or essèssè) are sold at African grocery stores. If you are unable to find them, you can replace these spices with ground nutmeg for djansang, cloves for the pèbè, and curry powder for the prekese.

YASSA CHICKEN

DIFFICULTY: MEDIUM • PREPARATION: 40 MINUTES + OVERNIGHT MARINATING • COOKING: 45 MINUTES

INGREDIENTS
FOR 4 PEOPLE

3 lb 5 oz (1.5 kg) free-range chicken

1 lb 2 oz (500 g) white onions

10 lemons

2 tbsp red nokoss (see p. 26)

2 tbsp mustard

Salt and pepper

2½ tbsp olive oil

1 bouquet garni (a tied bundle of herbs such as parsley, bay leaves, and thyme)

PREPARATION

For a better result, marinate the chicken a day ahead.

Rinse the chicken and pat dry, then cut it into pieces. Peel and finely chop the onions. Zest and juice the lemons.

Place two-thirds of the red nokoss in a bowl and mix in the mustard and lemon zest. Liberally brush the chicken pieces with the marinade. Pour half the lemon juice over the chicken (reserve the rest of the juice for cooking) and mix in the chopped onion. Season with salt and pepper, then cover and refrigerate overnight.

On the day of serving, separate the chicken from the onion (don't throw out the marinade). Working in batches if necessary, cook the chicken pieces in a large sauté pan with half the olive oil until browned on both sides. Set the browned chicken pieces aside.

Add the remaining oil to the same pan the chicken was browned in, add the onion, and gently sweat over medium heat for 15 minutes. Add the reserved lemon juice, remaining nokoss, bouquet garni, and marinade. Adjust the seasoning if required. Cook over low heat for 15 minutes. Add the chicken pieces and 1 cup (250 ml) water, then cover and simmer over medium heat for 15 minutes.

Serve the chicken on a large platter with white rice.

CHEF ANTO'S TIP

Yassa chicken is originally from Casamance in Senegal. Traditionally it is a dish of sautéed chicken with onions and lemon. Nowadays, there are versions that contain green olives, white vinegar instead of lemon, or even barbecued meat. To get the onions to really melt in the mouth, choose white onions or scallions. Finally, in Africa, meat is cooked with the bones, so if you want to keep with tradition, forget about using boneless chicken breasts!

FISH IN BANANA LEAF

DIFFICULTY: EASY • PREPARATION : 30 MINUTES • COOKING: 30 MINUTES

INGREDIENTS
FOR 4 PEOPLE

1 large oily fish such as catfish, emperor, mackerel, or salmon, around 3 lb 5 oz (1.5 kg)

2 white onions

2 tomatoes

1 bunch Guinea sorrel leaves (see tips p. 140, 192)

4 banana leaves

4 tsp green nokoss (see p. 26)

4 red chiles

2 country onions (see tip) or garlic cloves

2 lemons

Salt and pepper

PREPARATION

Preheat the oven to 300°F (150°C).

Scale and clean the fish. Rinse the fish and cut it into four pieces.

Peel and thinly slice the onions. Cut the tomatoes in half and slice into half rounds. Pick and finely chop the sorrel leaves.

Cut the banana leaves in half. Lay two half banana leaves in a deep plate to form a cross shape. Place a piece of fish on top and add a quarter of the tomato and onion slices, 1 tsp of the green nokoss, a quarter of the chopped sorrel, 1 whole chile, half a country onion, and the juice of half a lemon. Season with salt and pepper and close the leaves to make a parcel. Secure with kitchen twine. Repeat to make three more fish parcels.

Pour 1 cup (250 ml) water into a baking dish. Add the fish parcels and bake for 30 minutes.

CHEF ANTO'S TIP

Oily fish such as emperor fish, mackerel, catfish, or even salmon are the best to use for these parcels. They are rich in fatty acids, and the fish won't dry out quickly during cooking. If you don't have banana leaves, foil will also work well.

"Country onions," as they are called in Ghana and Nigeria, or "rondelles" in Cameroon, "bobimbi" in the Congo, and "sinzakolo" in Gabon, are the dried nut of a tropical forest plant and impart dishes with a garlicky black truffle flavor. (Pictured on p. 20.)

AFRICAN SALAD BOWL

DIFFICULTY: EASY • PREPARATION: 30 MINUTES • COOKING: NONE

INGREDIENTS
FOR 4 PEOPLE

1 cup (100 g) millet semolina

Olive oil

2 lemons

Salt and pepper

1½ cups (50 g) baby spinach leaves

1 stem of cherry tomatoes on the vine, halved

½ avocado, sliced

¼ red cabbage, thinly sliced

¼ semi-ripe papaya, diced

½ red onion, thinly sliced

1 mild/sweet chile, thinly sliced

⅓ cup (50 g) cooked black-eyed peas (see tip p. 50)

1¾ oz (50 g) African pistachios (egusi, see tip p. 116) or raw pumpkin seeds

PREPARATION

Pour the millet semolina into a bowl and add one 1 tbsp of olive oil. Wet the semolina by gradually adding about ½ cup (120 ml) of salted cold water and rolling the semolina between the palms of your hands. Make sure you smooth out any lumps that form.

Cook the semolina by steaming it in a steamer basket. Set a timer for 20 minutes from when the steam starts to pass through the semolina.

Juice the lemons into a bowl, then whisk in enough olive oil to make a dressing. Season with salt and pepper and mix well.

Arrange all the salad ingredients on a plate: the semolina, spinach, tomato halves, avocado slices, cabbage, papaya, onion, chile, and black-eyed peas.

Pour the dressing over the salad, sprinkle with the African pistachios, and enjoy.

CHEF ANTO'S TIP

Africa is packed with so much varied produce that it is easy to make all kinds of salad bowls for any kind of dietary requirement. You can substitute any ingredient if needed—the only one you need is creativity!

SAVORY FISH WITH EGGPLANTS

DIFFICULTY: MEDIUM • PREPARATION: 20 MINUTES + OVERNIGHT SOAKING • COOKING: 40 MINUTES

INGREDIENTS
FOR 6 PEOPLE

4 lb 8 oz (2 kg) salt cod

10½ oz (300 g) African or other small eggplants

2 carrots

3½ oz (100 g) okra

6 firm tomatoes

3 tbsp red palm oil

2 tbsp orange nokoss (see p. 27)

1 bouquet garni (a tied bundle of herbs such as parsley, bay leaves, and thyme)

Salt and pepper

¼ bunch flat-leaf parsley

PREPARATION

Soak the cod in a large bowl of cold water overnight or for at least 8 hours to desalt it. Change the water regularly.

Cook the eggplants in salted boiling water for 20 minutes. Leave to cool, then remove the stems and peel the eggplants. Cut the eggplants in half and set aside in a cool place.

Drain the cod, then scale it, and cut it into pieces.

Peel the carrots and cut them into rounds. Cut the okra in half lengthways and cut the tomatoes into large cubes.

Heat the red palm oil in a Dutch oven or heavy pot. Add the orange nokoss and sweat for 3 minutes. Add the cod pieces and stir, then add the carrot and tomatoes. Cover with water, add the bouquet garni, and simmer over medium heat for 10 minutes.

Add the eggplant and okra, adjust the seasoning if needed, then reduce the heat and simmer for 10 minutes.

Finely chop the parsley and sprinkle it on the fish before serving.

CHEF ANTO'S TIP

Called "makayabu" in the Congo Basin, salted fish is very popular in the Central African regions, where there are many waterways and rivers. Properly desalting the fish is essential to getting this dish right. It's preferable to do this the day before or in the morning for the evening and you need to change the soaking water regularly (every 30 minutes if possible).

WAATCHI

DIFFICULTY: MEDIUM • PREPARATION: 20 MINUTES + 4 HOURS SOAKING • COOKING: 2 MINUTES

INGREDIENTS
FOR 4 PEOPLE

½ cup (100 g) dried red kidney beans

¼ cup (60 ml) oil (canola, sunflower, or peanut)

2 tbsp red nokoss (see p. 26)

2 tsp tomato paste

1 cup (200 g) parboiled long-grain rice

Salt and pepper

1 bouquet garni (a tied bundle of herbs such as parsley, bay leaves, and thyme)

PREPARATION

Soak the dried beans in plenty of water for at least 4 hours (or overnight).

Drain the beans, rinse in clean water, and drain again. Cook the beans in a covered pot of salted boiling water for 1 hour or until tender.

In a large pot, heat the oil over high heat and sweat the nokoss for 3 minutes. Add the tomato paste and drained beans, then cook over medium heat for 10 minutes, stirring constantly.

Add the rice, salt, and pepper and mix everything together. Pour in about 1¼ cups (300 ml) water or enough to cover the ingredients. Add the bouquet garni and bring to a boil, then cook for 5 minutes.

Reduce the heat to the lowest setting, then cover and simmer for 20 minutes.

Serve the rice and beans with a spicy tomato sauce.

Born in 1968 in Ouagadougou, in Burkina Faso, Seydou Boro was a soccer player before becoming an actor and performer. He joined Mathilde Monnier's company at the National Center for Choreography in Montpellier in 1993 and was involved in several of the company's creations. In 1995, Seydou Boro joined forces with Salia Sanou and created the Salia nï Seydou company. Their first work, *Le Siècle des fous*, was performed in 1996 and sat between African tradition and contemporary gestural choreography. Boro and Sanour both embody originality and creativity and are part of a new generation of choreographers in Africa seeking to break with exotic stereotypes of traditional dance.

The Salia nï Seydou company has created 11 shows that have been performed in France and overseas. At the same time, Seydou Boro

In 2010, after many years of working together, Seydou Boro and Salia Sanou suspended their company in order to return to performing individually. They continued to co-direct and manage the art direction of La Termitière. In 2010, Seydou Boro released his first album, *Kanou*, and also founded Corps d'Hommes—Company Seydou Boro. In 2011, he created *Le Tango du Cheval*, a piece for seven dancers and three musicians. In 2012, he created a show in Ouagadougou, *Pourquoi la hyène a les pattes inférieures plus courtes que celles de devant et le singe les fesses pelées? (Why does a hyena have shorter back than front legs and a monkey have a bare bottom?).*

In 2015, Seydou Boro was named Commander in the Order of Arts and Letters by the French Minister for Culture and, in recognition of his musical career, was awarded the Francophone

SEYDOU

also filmed documentaries on creative African dance: *La Rencontre* and *La Danseuse d'ébène* (which won first prize Vues d'Afrique international film festival in 2003). Seydou Boro also worked with Récréatrales in Ouagadougou, Tof Théâtre in Brussels (puppets), and collaborated with Bakary Sangaré, from the Comédie-Française, to adapt a script that he wrote in 2002, *L'Exil dans l'asile*. In 2004, he produced *C'est ça l'Afrique*, *Visas*, *Le Cheval*, *On s'en fou*, and *La Fissure*, short fictional dance-themed films. In 2006, he acted in one of the shorts produced by Oliver Schmitz for the film *Paris, je t'aime*. Seydou Boro and Salia Sanou are also art directors of La Termitière, the Ouagadougou Center for Choreographic Development.

Regions Music prize at the Musiques métisses festival in Angoulême. In 2016, he created *Le Cri de la chair*, for five dancers and two musicians, then, with Salia Sanou and Irène Tassembédo, he co-directed the dance triennal *Afrique Danse!* in conjuction with the *Institut français* in Ouagadougou.

In 2018, Seydou Boro released his second album, *Hôrôn*, recorded in Burkina Faso and produced by Christian Mousset for Label Bleu—Maison de la culture d'Amiens. The group has been touring since April 2018. In September 2019, Seydou Boro created and performed the solo show *Kotéba*.

www.seydouboro.com
www.facebook.com/seydouborocompagnie

What are your favorite Sub-Saharan African dishes? A star ingredient?

My favorite dish has always been tô (cornmeal dough balls) and okra sauce with meat. When I am on tour and have the opportunity to return to Burkina Faso, my mother knows that if she wants to make me happy, then she has to cook tô with okra sauce. If it's made with meat, it's usually mutton, but it can also be made with fish. In Burkina there are a lot of fish (freshwater, of course!), such as carp. If I get a morning flight, then it's highly likely that my mother has prepared this dish for dinner. She likes making this dish!

Does this trigger a taste memory, like Proust's madeleine?

There is a lot of diversity in our dishes, but this dish in particular always makes me think of my mother. When I am in Paris in an African restaurant and I order tô, I immediately think of my "old lady" ("old lady" is a term of endearment in my country) and my thoughts are directly transported to my mother's place. This dish really takes me back to my childhood. Nowadays, there are quite a few ingredients added that my mother didn't use back then. She cooked in a very simple way—plain, but very rich. There weren't necessarily many different flavors, but it was very good. I love the sticky sauce with meat like mutton or also with fish. Just talking about it makes my mouth water!

What is your connection to this cuisine now?

I have now been living in France for 25 years and eat this dish much less frequently since I've been here. Although I cook, I have never been able to make it well—I've never achieved exactly the same flavors! Sometimes I use semolina bought here that I cobble together with okra, but it doesn't look anything like what my mother used to make. It's just a poor imitation and nothing like the original. I actually ate tô with okra sauce for lunch today with a friend from Burkina Faso. It's not really an iconic dish from Burkina Faso, because it can also be found in Senegal, Mali, and the Ivory Coast; it's the basic dish for many families in West Africa. It can be made with other flours like millet, for example, but I prefer it with cornmeal.

Do you have a tip, a short recipe, or any cooking advice?

Oh, no, I'm not the right person to give advice! Sometimes at home I make mafé (with peanut butter) and rice. But often I improvise, to make what I feel like on the day.

When I arrived in France, I worked at the Choreographic Center in Montpellier for ten years, and there was no one to make meals for me. Unlike in Burkina, where it was my mother or my sisters who cooked, when I came here I was forced to start cooking for myself. Salia [Salia Sanou, colleague and choreographer] and I just cobbled things together in the kitchen. We started with pasta because it was the easiest and fastest to make, then we gradually moved to more complex sauces, but it really was quite tentative at the start, mixing together ingredients based on memories of what we'd seen. Then the next time, we would change things a bit because what we'd made the night before was actually not that great! So, I really learned by myself as I went along, by improvising. It's like when I'm looking for a movement in dance; cooking is something that comes intuitively to me. But with time and experience, my cooking is better than it was when I started out ... at least I hope it is!

> When I am on tour and have the opportunity to return to Burkina Faso, my mother knows that if she wants to make me happy, then she has to cook tô with okra sauce.

CASSAVA LEAVES WITH PEANUT BUTTER

DIFFICULTY: MEDIUM • PREPARATION: 20 MINUTES • COOKING: 1 HOUR 40 MINUTES

INGREDIENTS
FOR 6 PEOPLE

2 lb 4 oz (1 kg) crushed cassava leaves

Salt and pepper

1 smoked mackerel

3 tbsp green nokoss (see p. 26)

2 tbsp sunflower oil

1 country onion (see tip p. 86)

10½ oz (300 g) red palm butter (see tip p. 106)

Scant ½ cup (100 g) smooth unsalted peanut butter

PREPARATION

Place the crushed cassava leaves in a pot and cover with water. Add 1 tsp salt and bring to a boil. Cook for 1 hour or until the liquid has completely evaporated.

Meanwhile, remove the skin from the mackerel. Flake the meat into pieces using your hands and remove any bones.

In a frying pan, sweat the nokoss in the sunflower oil. Add the mackerel and country onion. Cook for 5 minutes, then set aside.

When the cassava leaves are cooked, add the palm butter, then reduce the heat and simmer for 15 minutes. Add the mackerel mixture. Whisk the peanut butter with a little water to thin it out, then stir it into the cassava leaves. Adjust the seasoning if required, then simmer for 20 minutes.

Serve with rice or steamed root vegetables.

CHEF ANTO'S TIP

Across the African continent, the principle for this dish stays the same, with a few variations and many names. It is called saka saka (Democratic Republic of the Congo), pundu (Republic of the Congo, Angola), ngoundja (Central African Republic), kwem (Cameroon), ravitoto (Madagascar), matapa (Mozambique), mataba (Comoros), etodjey (Senegal), and sauce with cassava leaves in one part of West Africa.

The consistency of cassava leaves varies from one country to another. In some countries, this dish will have the consistency of a sauce, in others it will resemble a spinach side dish. In any case, the cassava leaves are better the day after they are prepared and the flavors of each ingredient have had time to mature. It's possible to replace the palm butter with cream or coconut milk, and to use pieces of meat or crustaceans instead of smoked fish.

PEANUT-CRUSTED CHICKEN

(my version of mafé)

DIFFICULTY: MEDIUM · PREPARATION: 45 MINUTES
COOKING: 1 HOUR 20 MINUTES + 2 HOURS RESTING TIME

INGREDIENTS
FOR 4 PEOPLE

3 lb 5 oz (1.5 kg) free-range whole chicken, or 2 lb (910 g) boneless breasts and thighs plus some bones for the sauce

1 lemon

1 tbsp red nokoss (see p. 26)

Salt and pepper

3 tbsp vegetable oil

FOR THE CRUST

⅓ cup (50 g) roasted peanuts

½ cup (50 g) dried breadcrumbs

Salt and pepper

2 eggs, beaten

Scant ½ cup (50 g) all-purpose flour

FOR THE SAUCE

3 tbsp vegetable oil

2 tbsp red nokoss (see p. 26)

3 tbsp peanut butter

1 mild/sweet chile

Salt and pepper

PREPARATION

Clean the chicken the day before, or at least 2 hours prior to cooking, and separate the breast and thigh meat from the bones. Set the bones aside for the sauce. Juice the lemon.

Coat the boneless chicken pieces with the lemon juice and nokoss and season with salt and pepper. Leave to marinate in the fridge.

To make the sauce, break up the chicken bones. Heat the oil in a pot and sweat the red nokoss for 3 minutes. Add the chicken bones and brown for 20 minutes over medium heat.

Stir the peanut butter and 2 cups (500 ml) water into the red nokoss mixture. Add the whole chile and simmer over low heat for 30 minutes. The sauce will gradually thicken. Season to taste and remove the bones.

For the crust, finely crush the roasted peanuts and put them on a plate with the breadcrumbs and a pinch of salt and pepper. Mix well. In a shallow bowl, mix the beaten eggs with 1 tbsp water. Put the flour on another plate. Coat the chicken pieces in the flour, then dip in the beaten eggs and coat with the peanut breadcrumbs.

Preheat the oven to 300°F (150°C).

Heat the oil in a large frying pan and brown the chicken pieces. Transfer the chicken to a baking pan and bake in the oven for 30 minutes or until cooked through.

Serve the chicken and sauce with rice, plantain fufu (page 130), or cassava tubers cooked in water.

PÈPÈ SOUP
(fish and crustacean soup)

DIFFICULTY: EASY • PREPARATION: 40 MINUTES + 2 HOURS CHILLING TIME • COOKING: 20 MINUTES

INGREDIENTS
FOR 4 PEOPLE

1 bunch green onions or scallions (white parts)

½ bunch Guinea sorrel leaves (see tips p. 140, 192)

3½ oz (100 g) okra

4 sea bream

4 large shell-on jumbo shrimp

4 crab pincers

4 tbsp green nokoss (see p. 26)

4 tsp red palm oil

1 cup (150 g) cherry tomatoes with stems

1 tbsp dried smoked shrimp powder

6 mild/sweet chiles

1 country onion (see tip) or garlic clove

Salt and pepper

PREPARATION

Cut the green onions or scallions into chunks. Pick and finely chop the sorrel leaves. Trim the ends of the okra.

Scale the fish and gut them through the head, then rinse and cut in half. Peel the shrimp, keeping the heads and tails intact. Break the crab pincers and peel carefully. Season the fish, shrimp, and crab pincers with 2 tbsp of the green nokoss. Set aside in the fridge for at least 2 hours (ideally overnight).

Heat the red palm oil in a pot. Brown the green onions with the remaining green nokoss. Add the tomatoes, then cover and simmer for 5 minutes. Add the fish pieces, shrimp, crab pincers, shrimp powder, chopped sorrel, whole chiles, country onion, and okra. Pour in 2 cups (500 ml) water, season with salt and pepper, then cover and simmer over low heat for 15 minutes, gently turning the fish pieces over halfway through cooking.

Serve the soup with cassava bread or fufu.

CHEF ANTO'S TIP

Pèpè soup is a stock. Traditionally, we use what we have on hand: offal, meat, fish, mollusks, and/or crustaceans. The cooking time will depend on the ingredients and, in this case, the size of the fish. You can use mild chiles if you don't like spicy dishes.

Country onions, as they are called in Ghana, are also called "bobimbi" in the Congo, "rondelles" in Cameroon, and "sinzakolo" in Gabon. They come from the fruit of the garlic tree and are used as a condiment in the preparation of several sauces, and are also used in traditional medicine. (Pictured p. 20.)

ODIKA SMOKED CHICKEN

DIFFICULTY: MEDIUM • PREPARATION: 30 MINUTES • COOKING: 1 HOUR

INGREDIENTS
FOR 4 PEOPLE

3 lb 5 oz (1.5 kg) smoked chicken

1¾ oz (50 g) okra

7 oz (200 g) odika seeds (African bush mango seeds, see tip)

Vegetable oil

3 tbsp red nokoss (see p. 26)

Salt and pepper

1 mild/sweet chile

PREPARATION

Clean the chicken and cut it into pieces.

Trim the ends of the okra. Blanch the okra for 5 minutes in salted boiling water. Drain and set aside.

Toast the odika seeds in a large sauté pan over medium heat until they are nicely golden. Remove from the heat and, using a mortar and pestle, crush the hot seeds until they form a smooth, chocolate-colored paste. Set aside.

In the same pan, brown the chicken pieces all over in a little oil. Remove the chicken from the pan and set aside.

Cook the odika paste in the sauté pan over medium heat for 5 minutes. Add the red nokoss and cook, stirring constantly, for 5 minutes. Pour in 2 cups (500 ml) water and season with salt and pepper. Bring the sauce to a boil and simmer for 30 minutes.

Add the chicken pieces and simmer for 10 minutes until cooked through, then add the okra and whole chile at the end.

CHEF ANTO'S TIP

Odika comes from a type of wild mango that grows in the forests of Gabon. It is made by breaking open the mango seed and removing the inner kernel. The kernel is then dried and dry roasted. In Gabon, it is traditionally crushed while still hot in order to preserve it. The paste is placed in molds and left to cool. You can then grate off what you need from the block of odika. This seed is already oil-rich, which is why we don't add any additional oil. Odika goes by several different names: "nfiang ndo'o" in Cameroon, "ndimba" in the Congo, and "ogbono soup" in Nigeria. Some even call it "native chocolate," except that odika only has the color and smell of chocolate. Toasting the seeds is a very important step. If they are burnt, you will taste it in the sauce, so it's important to watch the intensity of the heat. To get around this problem, you can find ready-to-use blocks of odika in African grocery stores. In this case, all you need to do is grate off what you need. This odika sauce is a perfect accompaniment to meat and smoked fish. You can use frozen okra if you can't find fresh.

CHAKALAKA
(spicy vegetables and beans)

DIFFICULTY: EASY • PREPARATION: 25 MINUTES + 4 HOURS SOAKING • COOKING: 1 HOUR 30 MINUTES

INGREDIENTS
FOR 6 PEOPLE

1¼ cups (250 g) dried white beans

1¼ cups (250 g) dried chickpeas

1 red onion

2 Roma tomatoes

1 red sweet pepper

2 carrots

Vegetable oil

2 tbsp orange nokoss (see p. 27)

2 tsp Madras curry powder

1 tsp paprika

1 tsp thyme leaves

Salt and pepper

PREPARATION

Soak the dried beans and chickpeas separately in water for at least 4 hours, or overnight.

Drain the beans and chickpeas, then rinse them in clean water and drain again.

Cook the beans and chickpeas separately in covered pots of salted boiling water for 1 hour or until tender.

Peel and finely chop the onion. Finely dice the tomatoes and sweet pepper. Peel and grate the carrots.

Heat a little oil in a large pot, then sweat the orange nokoss with the onion until it becomes translucent. Add the curry powder, paprika, and thyme and cook, stirring, for 2 minutes. Add the tomato, sweet pepper, and carrots, then cover and cook over low heat for 20 minutes, stirring occasionally.

Add the cooked beans and chickpeas, season with salt and pepper, and cook for a further 5 minutes. Serve hot or cold.

Chakalaka is ideal as a vegetarian meal or as a side for a barbecue.

SAUTÉED OKRA WITH MUSHROOMS

DIFFICULTY: EASY • PREPARATION: 15 MINUTES • COOKING: 30 MINUTES

INGREDIENTS FOR 4 PEOPLE

10½ oz (300 g) okra

5½ oz (150 g) chanterelle mushrooms

2 white onions

Vegetable oil

3 tbsp green nokoss (see p. 26)

1 tbsp peanut butter

2 habanero chiles

PREPARATION

Trim the ends of the okra, then cut it into rounds. Chop the mushrooms. Peel and finely chop the onions.

Heat a little oil in a pot over medium heat. Sweat the nokoss, mushrooms, and onions for around 2 minutes.

Add the peanut butter and stir for 3 minutes. Add the okra rounds and 2 cups (500 ml) water, then simmer over low heat for 20 minutes. Add the whole chiles 5 minutes before the end of cooking.

Enjoy this vegetarian dish with white rice or fufu.

CHEF ANTO'S TIP

Contrary to what many people think, there are a great number of vegetarian and vegan dishes in African cuisines. Also, given that the equatorial regions of Africa are very humid, many kinds of mushrooms, such as chanterelles, oyster, and black trumpet can be found. If you can't find fresh okra, you can use dried okra powder or blanched and chopped okra leaves.

NILE PERCH NYEMBWE

DIFFICULTY: MEDIUM • PREPARATION: 30 MINUTES • COOKING: 45 MINUTES

INGREDIENTS
FOR 4 PEOPLE

3½ oz (100 g) okra

3 scallions

Vegetable oil for deep-frying

2 lb 4 oz (1 kg) Nile perch, sea bass, or barramundi fillets

Salt and pepper

All-purpose flour, for coating

3 tbsp orange nokoss (see p. 27)

14 oz (400 g) red palm butter (see tip p. 96)

1 tbsp dried shrimp powder

10½ oz (300 g) crabs, halved

2 green chiles

Baby spinach leaves

PREPARATION

Cut the okra in half lengthways and cut the scallions into quarters.

Heat the oil for deep-frying.

Clean the fish. Cut the fillets in half, season with salt and pepper, and coat with flour. Working in batches, deep-fry the fish pieces in the hot oil until golden. Drain on paper towels and set aside.

Sweat the nokoss and 1 tbsp of the palm butter in a large Dutch oven or heavy pot for 2 minutes. Add the shrimp powder and crabs and cook, stirring constantly, for 5 minutes.

Add the remaining palm butter, season with salt and pepper, and simmer over low heat for 10 minutes.

Add the okra, scallions, and whole chiles, then cover and simmer for 10 minutes. Add the fried fish pieces and some water, if needed, and simmer for 10 minutes.

To serve, remove the fish pieces, crabs, and vegetables from the pot. Briefly whisk the sauce, then pour it into a serving dish. Arrange the fish, crabs, and vegetables on top. Decorate with a few baby spinach leaves and serve with steamed root vegetables.

CHEF ANTO'S TIP

Nyembwe (as we call it in Gabon), is called "sauce graine" in the Ivory Coast, "moambé" in the Congo, and "banga soup" in Nigeria. It is made from the pulp of the oil palm kernel (also sometimes labeled red palm butter, or palmnut cream or concentrate). This sauce is also a wonderful accompaniment to meat and smoked fish. If you can't source palm kernel pulp, you can use cream or coconut milk.

Poet, slam poet, and novelist Marc Alexandre Oho Bambe, called Captain Alexandre, spreads notes and words of resistance and peace, of memory and hope. Writing from the heart, his poems and steps are guided by mentors who have taught him to think and hope. His poetry sings of the possible, the gift of oneself, of love and revolt, the quest to be human, "nothing but human," and the radical refusal to live "with arms crossed in the sterile attitude of a spectator."

Captain Alexandre has published seven books: *ADN. Afriques Diasporas Négritude*, La Plume de l'Ange, 2009; *Le Chant des possibles*, La Cheminante, 2014 (Fetkann poetry prize and Paul Verlaine poetry prize awarded by the Académie-Française in 2015); *Résidents de la République*, La Cheminante, 2016; *De terre, de mer, d'amour et de feu*, Mémoire d'Encrier, 2017 (City of Valognes prize in 2018); *Diên Biên Phù*, Sabine Wespieser publisher, 2018 (Louis Guilloux prize in 2018,

Chambéry winner of best novel and Roblès prize in 2019); *Ci-gît mon cœur-poème*, La Cheminante, 2018; *Fragments*, Éditions Bernard Chauveau, 2019.

A founding member of the On A Slamé Sur La Lune collective, Captain Alexandre also writes articles (*Africultures*, *Médiapart*, *Le Nouveau Magazine littéraire*) and presents at schools and universities, where he teaches students respect and meaning, a spirit of curiosity for the Other and free existence, liberated from dogmas and extremes.

Marc Alexandre Oho Bambe was made a Knight in the National Order of Merit by presidential order on May 2, 2017.

Captain Alexandre slams his poetry and sings of possibility on stages worldwide.

CAPTAIN

For more information:
www.capitainealexandre.com

ALEXANDRE

J'AI L'*AFRIQUE*
DANS LES VEINES

L'AFRIQUE
DANS LES Gènes

C'EST UNE HISTOIRE
D'*ADN*

ET TANT PIS
SI *ça gêne*

J'AI L'AFRIQUE
AU *cœur*

JE LA PORTE
EN MOI

PARTOUT *Où* JE *VAIS Où je vibre*

DANS MES *SOURIRES*
ET MES *larmes*

DANS MA VOIX QUI SILENCE
ET MES MOTS QUI LA CHANTENT

AFRIQUE, ô MON AFRIQUE

...

Marc Alexandre Oho Bambe
Dit Capitaine Alexandre

What are your favorite Sub-Saharan African dishes? A star ingredient?

Two dishes spring naturally to mind. First of all, ndolé, but not just any, the one my grandmother makes! A real delight for the taste buds, but also for the soul, memories of Sundays spent with family at home, with my grandparents, uncles, aunts, parents, and my brother and sister. A table and an image of eternal love. My entire childhood in Douala is connected to this dish that my grandmother made like no one else. This is normally a coastal dish, but it is true that ndolé is loved unanimously in Cameroon, and finding something unanimous in this country is already something! (*Laughs.*)

The second dish that comes to mind is mafé, but it has to be chicken mafé! I had never eaten it in Cameroon but tasted it for the first time in Lille, in the north of France, with some African friends from university. We often went to each other's houses and we not only discovered each other's cultures, but also just how diverse Africa actually is—in its languages, its cuisine, its expressions, and in its humor.

What we knew in theory, we fully experienced through meeting others. Then, as I performed concerts in Senegal and the Ivory Coast, I continued on a journey discovering other tastes of Africa.

My star ingredient is mango! Mango is life! (*Laughs.*) There was a mango tree at my grandparents' place and I remember spending nights listening to the mangoes fall. The next morning I was the first to run out to make sure I collected the ripest ones. A ripe mango, and I mean a tropical mango, is absolute bliss!

Does this trigger a taste memory, like Proust's madeleine?

Yes, taste can bring your whole childhood back to the surface. Even today, eating ndolé at my aunt's takes me back to Bonapriso, even though my aunt lives in France. Eating a good ndolé transports me back 25 years. I can see my grandmother's hands preparing the meal and I'm back in my happy childhood place.

And mangoes, well, they taught me a lot about patience. This was because we were young mango thieves. We didn't always wait for them to fall from the tree and would get in trouble from my grandfather who said we needed to learn to wait and accept things as they come, rather than wanting to pick them. It was actually teaching us about philosophy and wisdom, to never race ahead but to always wait for the right time to enjoy the moment.

My strongest food memories are associated with mangoes and ndolé. (*Laughs.*)

You never eat well if you eat alone: special memories are created when you eat with others, the people you share a meal with, whether it's your family or friends who are like brothers, such as Fred Ebami. Sharing mangoes before or after our street soccer games in Bonapriso, the suburb where we grew up, is one of those indescribable moments that cemented our friendship.

At my grandmother's place, ndolé was always served with missolés—plantains. Of all the food on earth, plantains are surely the one I ate most during my childhood. I ate them in the morning, at midday, and in the evening. Missolés go wonderfully with ndolé. Actually I advise everyone to eat a plate of ndolé and missolés at least once in their life. (*Smiles.*)

> You never eat well if you eat alone: special memories are created when you eat with others, the people you share a meal with, whether it's your family or friends who are like brothers.

What is your connection to this cuisine now?

I don't cook a great deal—I usually make simple things—but I do find there are similarities between cooking and writing—the different ingredients, for example. It was Dany Laferrière who made me see this. Cooking and writing also share the same sense of waiting and intuition. We have all the ingredients to write a novel, the characters, the story, and you need to put it all together in a pot, bring it to a boil ... and only take everything out of the pot when the meal is perfectly cooked. It is only then that you serve up your story. I really like this literary image of cooking.

When you cook, you find some of that same intuition in the ingredients and recipes. Some people follow a recipe precisely, whereas others, the artists and creative types, let intuition take over. They end up making something that surprises themselves, and perhaps surprises others too.

Do you have a tip, a short recipe, or any cooking advice?

A recipe with sliced chicken in sauce and missolés. I've changed the DG chicken recipe a bit, but that's also intuition coming into play, changing things to make them your own. So, sliced chicken in curry sauce and missolés, a mix of flavors and combining tastes of Africa, India, and Asia in one dish. Taking you on a journey with spices not normally used in African cooking, well, at least not the African cuisine I ate as a child. Your mouth explodes with flavors, which in the end just makes us feel like we belong to the world: we no longer know if we're eating an African dish or an Indian dish, we just know that we are actually eating THE WORLD! Let's eat the world! (*Laughs.*)

THIEP BOU DIEN

DIFFICULTY: MEDIUM • PREPARATION : 1 HOUR • COOKING: 1 HOUR 30 MINUTES

INGREDIENTS
FOR 6 TO 8 PEOPLE

4 lb 8 oz (2 kg) white grouper

6 tbsp green nokoss
(see p. 26)

Vegetable oil for deep-frying

3½ oz (100 g) pumpkin or
squash

2 carrots

1 turnip

1 cassava tuber

6 African or other small
eggplants

½ white cabbage

2 tbsp tomato paste

8 cups (2 liters) fish stock

Salt and pepper

1 fresh chile

1 tsp soumbala (see tip p. 26)

7 oz (200 g) tamarind paste

11½ cups (2 kg) broken white
rice

1 piece of guedjef and yété
(dried fish and shell) or dried
bonito flakes

FOR SERVING

Fresh herbs

Lime wedges

PREPARATION

Scale and clean the fish. Cut it into pieces and rinse in clean water. Make some reasonably deep cuts on the skin of each piece, then brush the fish with 2 tbsp of the green nokoss, ensuring some goes into the incisions. Heat enough oil for deep-frying, then fry each piece of fish and set aside.

Peel the pumpkin, carrots, turnip, and cassava. Cut all of the vegetables into large pieces.

In a large Dutch oven or heavy pot, brown 2 tbsp of the green nokoss with the tomato paste in a little oil. Cook over low heat for 3 minutes, then dilute with the fish stock. Add the vegetables and season with salt and pepper. Cover and simmer for 10 minutes. Add the whole chile, then simmer for 30 minutes.

Next make tamarind chutney: In a frying pan, brown 1 tbsp of the green nokoss with a drizzle of oil. Stir in the soumbala, then the tamarind paste. Season with salt and pepper, then cook until the mixture has reduced to resemble a chutney in texture. Set aside.

Meanwhile, rinse the broken rice in clean water. Bring some water to a boil in a couscoussier (or a steamer lined with cheesecloth) to partially cook the rice. Cover and cook the rice for 10 minutes.

Continued on p. 114.

THIEP BOU DIEN *recipe continued.*

Adjust the seasoning of the vegetables if required. Add the fish pieces to the pot, as well as the guedjef and yété, then simmer for 10 minutes. Remove the fish and vegetables from the pot and set aside. Strain the cooking liquid.

Pour half of the strained liquid and the broken rice into the Dutch oven (don't throw the rest of the liquid away—it is delicious). Bring to a boil, then reduce the heat and cook over very low heat for 15 minutes.

Add the final 1 tbsp green nokoss to the rice, mix, and finish cooking over low heat for 10 minutes. Fluff with a fork.

To serve, put the rice on a large serving platter and arrange the fish and vegetables on top. Add a few spoonfuls of the tamarind chutney. Decorate with the herbs and lime wedges.

CHEF ANTO'S TIP

Thiep bou dien (rice with fish) is the national dish of Senegal. In the introduction, I mentioned that prior to Africa being divided up in 1885, following the Berlin Conference, there were kingdoms. The kingdoms were also divided up. This is why, even if we say that thiep bou dien comes from Senegal, you can also find variants of it in the surrounding countries such as Mali, Gambia, or Mauritania.

Be careful not to cut the vegetables too small, otherwise they will end up disintegrating.

When cooking the rice in the sauce, the sauce needs to just cover the rice to avoid making a mush. It's better to add a bit of sauce if needed during cooking than start with too much.

In terms of choice of fish, it is preferable to use oily fish with firm flesh (Nile perch, emperor fish, or grouper), which will better hold their shape through the cooking process.

If you make this dish with meat, it is called "thiep bou yap" (rice with meat).

SAUTÉED BEEF WITH SPINACH SAUCE

DIFFICULTY: EASY • PREPARATION: 20 MINUTES + 1 HOUR CHILLING TIME • COOKING: 30 MINUTES

INGREDIENTS
FOR 4 PEOPLE

1 lb 2 oz (500 g) beef tenderloin

2 tbsp red nokoss (see p. 26)

1 lb 2 oz (500 g) English spinach

Splash of vinegar, for washing

3½ tbsp red palm oil

4 tbsp orange nokoss (see p. 27)

1 cup (100 g) ground African pistachios (egusi, see tip) or raw pumpkin seeds

Salt and pepper

FOR SERVING

A few mustard greens

Roasted African pistachios or pumpkin seeds

PREPARATION

Slice the beef into thin strips. Put the strips in a bowl with the red nokoss and mix well. Cover and set aside for 1 hour in the fridge.

Remove the stalks from the spinach. Wash the spinach leaves in vinegared water and then in clean water, swishing around well. Drain and set aside.

In a frying pan, heat half the red palm oil and sauté the beef in small batches for around 2 minutes or until well browned. Set aside.

In the same frying pan, sweat the orange nokoss with the remaining palm oil for 5 minutes. Add the spinach and sauté briefly, then add the ground African pistachios and stir for 5 minutes. Add a little water if it starts to stick. Add the beef slices and cooking juices and heat briefly. Season with salt and pepper.

Serve the sautéed beef and spinach with white rice. Garnish with a few mustard greens and roasted African pistachios.

CHEF ANTO'S TIP

This dish is a variation of égousi, a dish that is very popular in West Africa. It is generally eaten with offal, especially tripe, but if you are not a fan, steak will work really well.

African pistachios (pictured on p. 20) are nothing like the pistachios we are used to in the West. In Africa, what we call a pistachio is the almond-shaped kernel found in several types of squash, melon, or gourd. When these seeds are ground, they have the same properties as almond meal. In a pinch, you can use ground raw pumpkin seeds (your dish will have a slightly green color and the flavor will be milder).

SAUTÉED KIDNEYS WITH LENTILS

DIFFICULTY: MEDIUM • PREPARATION: 30 MINUTES • COOKING: 45 MINUTES

INGREDIENTS
FOR 6 PEOPLE

3 carrots

3 scallions

1 tomato

2 cups (400 g) green lentils

Salt and pepper

1 bouquet garni (a tied bundle of herbs such as parsley, bay leaves, and thyme)

7 oz (200 g) smoked streaky bacon

10½ oz (300 g) beef kidneys

2 tbsp orange nokoss (see p. 27)

Vegetable oil

Chervil sprigs, to serve

PREPARATION

Peel the carrots and cut them into rounds. Cut the scallions into quarters and finely dice the tomato.

Cover the lentils with cold water. Season with salt and pepper, then bring to a boil and cook for 10 minutes, then add the bouquet garni and the carrot rounds and continue to cook for 10 minutes.

Cut the bacon into strips. Remove the fat and veins from the kidneys, then cut them into cubes.

Fry the bacon in a hot Dutch oven or heavy pot. Add the kidneys, orange nokoss, and scallions and cook, stirring constantly, until browned. Add a drizzle of vegetable oil if needed.

Add the lentils and carrots to the pot with their cooking water. Taste and adjust the seasoning, then simmer over low heat for 10 minutes.

Serve, scattered with a few sprigs of chervil on top.

RABBIT KEDJENOU

DIFFICULTY: EASY • PREPARATION: 30 MINUTES • COOKING: 30 MINUTES

INGREDIENTS
FOR 4 PEOPLE

1 lb 10 oz (720 g) rabbit thighs

4 tbsp red nokoss
(see p. 26)

4 tsp red palm oil,
plus extra for drizzling

3 white onions

4 large tomatoes

2 eggplants

1 bunch flat-leaf parsley

1 bouquet garni (a tied bundle
of herbs such as parsley, bay
leaves, and thyme)

Salt and pepper

PREPARATION

Wash and trim the rabbit thighs. Combine the thighs with half of the red nokoss in a bowl.

Brown the rabbit thighs in the red palm oil in a Dutch oven or heavy pot. Remove and set aside.

Dice the onions and slice the tomatoes. Finely dice the eggplants and finely chop the parsley.

Sweat the remaining red nokoss in the Dutch oven, then place the rabbit thighs in the base and top with the onions, tomatoes, and eggplants. Add the bouquet garni and season with salt and pepper, then cover and simmer for 10 minutes.

Without removing the lid, vigorously shake the pot, then simmer over medium heat for another 10 minutes. Shake the pot a second time, then simmer for a further 10 minutes. It is very important not to remove the lid during cooking.

Serve hot with attiéké (cassava couscous).

CHEF ANTO'S TIP

Kedjenou means "shaken" in Baoulé language, a dialect spoken in the Ivory Coast.

The most popular kedjenou recipe is made with chicken, but this recipe is traditionally made with small game cooked in pieces over a wood fire in an earthenware dish called a "canari." This is a dish cooked without water using the "smothering" technique.

TUNA GARBA

DIFFICULTY: EASY · PREPARATION: 15 MINUTES · COOKING: 20 MINUTES

INGREDIENTS FOR 4 PEOPLE

2 white onions

4 large tomatoes

2 mild/sweet green chiles

1 lemon, halved

Salt

4 x 5½ oz (150 g) bluefin tuna steaks

Vegetable oil for deep-frying

Cilantro flowers (optional)

PREPARATION

Peel and finely chop the onions. Cut the tomatoes into quarters, remove the seeds, and finely dice the flesh.

Deseed and finely chop the chiles.

Put the onions, tomatoes, and chiles in a bowl and squeeze the lemon juice over the top. Set aside.

Salt the tuna steaks and deep-fry them in hot oil until crispy and cooked to your liking. Drain on paper towels.

Decorate the tuna steaks with the cilantro flowers (if using) and serve with the salad and attiéké (cassava couscous).

CHEF ANTO'S TIP

Tuna garba is the quick and inexpensive dish of choice of young people in Abidjan, the biggest city in Ivory Coast, and it is mainly cooked by Nigerian nationals. The term "garba" means "boy." The dish can also be called "attiéké-poisson," "zéguen," "foin," "guéro," "ganguatte," "béton dur," or "zeh."

In Europe and the West, fish is often eaten only just cooked, still pink on the bone, but in Africa fish is eaten well done, or even overcooked. This is true for tuna garba. The tuna can be replaced with tilapia or a grouper fillet in this recipe.

FOLONG RAVIOLI WITH SMOKED MACKEREL

DIFFICULTY: MEDIUM • PREPARATION: 1 HOUR • COOKING: 10 MINUTES

INGREDIENTS FOR 4 PEOPLE

7 oz (200 g) folong (amaranth leaves), plus extra to garnish (substitute chard)

1 small smoked mackerel, about 5½ oz (150 g)

3 tbsp red palm oil, plus extra for drizzling

2 tbsp green nokoss (see p. 26)

Salt and pepper

32 wonton wrappers

1 egg

All-purpose flour, for dusting

⅓ cup (50 g) roasted cashews

Scant 1 cup (200 ml) coconut milk

Scant 1 cup (200 ml) coconut cream

PREPARATION

Finely chop the amaranth leaves, setting a few aside for decoration.

To prepare the smoked mackerel, remove the head and skin, then flake the meat, removing all of the bones.

Heat the red palm oil in a frying pan and sweat the green nokoss, then drop in the amaranth leaves. Reduce the heat and cook for 5 minutes. Add the mackerel meat and season with salt and pepper. Transfer the amaranth leaves to a bowl and leave to cool.

Lay 16 wonton wrappers out on your work surface and put 1 tsp of the filling in the center of each. Using a fork, beat the egg in a bowl and brush the edges of the wrapper around the filling using a pastry brush. Cover with the other 16 wonton wrappers, pressing the edges to seal and remove any air. Cut out the ravioli using a cookie cutter and leave them to dry on a lightly floured plate.

Bring a large pot of salted water to a boil with a drizzle of red palm oil. Simmer the ravioli in batches for 2-3 minutes. Drain in a colander and divide among serving plates.

Roughly crush the roasted cashews. Heat the coconut milk and coconut cream in a saucepan. Season with salt and pepper. Just before serving, use a hand mixer to froth the coconut mixture. Skim off the froth using a soup spoon.

Serve the ravioli with the coconut mixture. Garnish with the reserved amaranth leaves and scatter with crushed cashews. Serve immediately.

SIDES

ΛLLOKOS
(fried plantains)

DIFFICULTY: EASY · PREPARATION: 10 MINUTES · COOKING: 20 MINUTES

INGREDIENTS
FOR 6 PEOPLE

6 very ripe plantains

Salt

Vegetable oil for deep-frying

PREPARATION

Peel the plantains and cut them into rounds (you don't need to scrape any bitter parts from very ripe plantains). Season the pieces with salt.

In a large pot, heat enough oil for deep-frying and, working in batches, deep-fry the plantain rounds for 2–3 minutes until both sides are golden.

Drain on paper towels and serve hot as a snack or as a side for grilled meat or fish.

CHEF ANTO'S TIP

The more black patches there are on a plantain, the sweeter it will be. The best places to find plantains are African, Indian, Latin American, or Caribbean grocery stores. Avoid buying them at supermarkets since they are generally not stored very well.

"Allokos" is the name for fried plantains in the Ivory Coast. While this is the name widely used today, fried plantains are traditionally called "missolés" in Cameroon; in Ghana and Nigeria, they are seasoned with spices and called "kéléwélé;" and they are called "maduros" in Equatorial Guinea.

PLANTAIN FUFU

DIFFICULTY: EASY · PREPARATION: 40 MINUTES · COOKING: 30 MINUTES

INGREDIENTS FOR 6 PEOPLE

4 ripe plantains

1 lb 2 oz (500 g) cassava tuber

3 tbsp red palm oil

PREPARATION

To peel the plantains, cut off the two ends, then use the tip of a knife to score the skin along the length of the plantain from one end to the other. Remove the skin. Using the back of a knife, gently scrape the flesh to remove the thin bitter layer. Cut them in half lengthways and remove the heart.

Peel the cassava using a knife, cut it in half lengthways, and remove the wooden stem in the center.

Rinse the cassava and plantains in water. Steam them in a couscoussier or a cheesecloth-lined steamer for 30 minutes. Keep the cassava warm while you prepare the plantain dough.

Using a large mortar and pestle, pound the plantains until a smooth dough forms, about 15 minutes. Pound the cassava separately, making sure the dough has no lumps.

Mix the two doughs together, then add the red palm oil and pound them together for 15 minutes. The fufu must be smooth.

Traditionally, fufu is served in an oval-shaped ball, similar to a football. Here I've used cookie and fondant cutters to give the fufu a more decorative shape and design.

CHEF ANTO'S TWIST

Depending on the country, we say "plantain futu" or "banana fufu." In my mother tongue, it is called "nkima."

Fufu is the perfect accompaniment to dishes with sauce.

Be careful when peeling the cassava. It cannot be peeled with a vegetable peeler, but needs to be peeled with a knife to properly remove the skin, which is poisonous if ingested. After peeling the cassava, you also need to remove the wooden stem in the middle as it is inedible.

RED RICE

DIFFICULTY: EASY · PREPARATION: 15 MINUTES · COOKING: 45 MINUTES

INGREDIENTS
FOR 6 PEOPLE

1½ cups (300 g) parboiled long-grain rice

¼ cup (60 ml) oil (canola, sunflower, or peanut)

2 tbsp red nokoss (see p. 26)

3 tbsp tomato paste

⅔ cup (150 g) tomato passata (puréed tomatoes)

2 Selim pepper pods

1 bay leaf

Salt

Chives, to serve

PREPARATION

Rinse the rice in cold water and drain. Pre-cook the rice for 10 minutes, either by steaming or in salted boiling water. Drain again.

Heat the oil in a large pot and sweat the nokoss for 3 minutes.

Add the tomato paste and cook over low heat for 6 minutes, stirring occasionally. Mix in the rice.

Add the passata, Selim pepper pods, and bay leaf and continue cooking until the mixture has reduced and thickened. Season with salt and add 2¼ cups (530 ml) water (or 1.5 times the volume of rice), then bring to a boil and cook for 3 minutes.

Reduce the heat to very low, then cover and cook for 10 minutes.

Stir the rice with a fork to separate the grains. Cover and leave to cook for a further 10 minutes. Repeat this step until the rice is cooked. Sprinkle with chopped chives.

Serve with grilled meat or dishes with meat and sauce.

CHEF ANTO'S TIP

Red rice in Central Africa is roughly the same as jollof rice or wolog rice in West Africa, or pilau rice in East Africa. This recipe is originally from Senegal but has as many variations as there are countries that claim it as their national dish. Each part of the continent has adapted the recipe according to its history, its environment, and the products that today make up its culinary identity.

To make this dish successfully, don't use round or basmati rice, or long-grain rice that hasn't been parboiled. You need a rice that remains firm when cooked and doesn't break up by absorbing the sauce during cooking. It's best to use jasmine rice or parboiled long-grain rice.

Red rice is always on the table at a celebration. It's an ideal side to spinach dishes, dishes with a sauce, and even grilled food.

Born in Benin in the 1970s, Patrick Ruffino is a bass player and singer. He grew up in Africa's capital of funk, Cotonou, which is also the birthplace of voodoo music and culture. He learned to play a multitude of instruments, and to sing and dance, and his thirst for discovery and love of travel brought him to France at the end of the 1980s. Still very attached to his roots, he continued to draw inspiration from Africa through several trips back to his home country.

Hailing from a multicultural family, with a father belonging to the Benin Mina ethnic group (double ethnicity is very common in Nigeria), a mother from Burkina Faso, and a grandmother from Ghana, from an early age Patrick was exposed to an environment that allowed him to experience a mix of all types of African music.

Patrick is always working and contributing to various projects as a director, composer, producer, and arranger. More recently, he has worked as artistic director on the Amazones d'Afrique project.

After a career spanning over 20 years in Africa, Europe, and the United States and a noteworthy debut album, Patrick released *Agoo*. His powerful and touching voice is perfectly suited to his vintage funk-rock style that echoes the performances of the early masters of highlife and Afro-beat. You can hear the strength of the percussion alongside the light funk gimmicks and sharp riffs reminiscent of seventies rock.

The traditional rhythms of Benin are not forgotten either; they are revamped in pieces that are both simple and complex at the same

PATRICK

Patrick's curiosity also led him to explore jazz, funk, soul, and Afro Cuban music. At the age of 10, he started to sing, then tried the bass player's guitar in his singing group—it has since become his instrument of choice.

In 1997, Patrick founded the group Fâ, with their album *Défi* receiving several awards in Benin. Since 2002, he has been performing as a solo artist and his album *E Wa Ka Jo* was named winner of RFI Discovery Prize for World Music in 2008.

time. This album also bears the mark of the voodoo tradition in Benin through the themes addressed in the song lyrics. In Yoruba, Fon, Mina, or Dendi (languages spoken in Benin), ancestors, certain codes of behavior, respect, and self-fulfillment are honored.

In this way, Patrick Ruffino invents unique popular music that is both clear and revolutionary, filled with a multitude of African and Western influences, but with its own solid and strong identity.

www.patrickruffino.com
www.facebook.com/PatrickRuffinoOfficial
www.instagram.com/patrickruffino.officiel

What are your favorite Sub-Saharan African dishes? A star ingredient?

My favorite dish is pounded yam. But there are several dishes that I like from Benin, where I'm from. There is a "red dough" made from cornmeal mixed with tomato sauce. There is also a "white dough" made from cornmeal. And "black dough" made with dried yams that are pounded into flour. There are also different spinach-based sauces.

But for today I will choose a simpler dish, "dried okra sauce." This dish is made from dried okra that is ground to make a flour, which is used to make the sauce. My favorite dish is pounded yam with dried okra sauce, accompanied by Fula cheese (called "wagashi" or "waragashi"), a cheese made by the Fula people in Benin's north.

Does this trigger a taste memory, like Proust's madeleine?

I am lucky enough to have four grandparents with diverse backgrounds: Benin, Ghana, Nigeria, and Burkina. My mother is originally from Burkina Faso. As a child of around 5 or 6 years old, I remember going with my mother to the north of Benin during the holidays to visit my grandmother, who used to make us this sauce with the pounded yams. I know how to make it and my sisters do as well, but when my mom makes it, it has a specific flavor.

Those were the holidays I spent as a small child, but then we grew up in more of an urban setting, in Cotonou and elsewhere. My father was a doctor and my mother was a diplomat and politician, so we traveled a lot.

What is your connection to this cuisine now?

I am still strongly connected to this cuisine. I love cooking and I know how to make several sauces from the sub-region of Benin. I also make some Western dishes. I love cooking, I love eating, I love to enjoy eating what I've made and also sharing it! It is such a wonderful thing to see the person or people you have cooked for appreciate what you have made. It's a bit like seeing that people are enjoying your music during a concert.

I would say that I am particularly attached to African cuisine as I mostly cook African dishes. I also like to experiment. Sometimes I prepare a dish in the way my mother or my sister would, but more often than not I experiment, always trusting my intuition, trying to get the right balance of flavors.

Do you have a tip, a short recipe, or any cooking advice?

I never use stock cubes! I use dried or ground shrimp to enhance a dish's flavor. I don't use white salt, but French sel gris. I use red or yellow onions, not white onions. I use organic tomatoes (in Africa, most of the vegetables are organic). I always use good-quality chicken, preferably free range. All of this adds a great deal of flavor to the dish. Buying good produce, good meat from a butcher, and good-quality fish from a fishmonger changes everything!

I rarely cook wheat semolina—I prefer to use cornmeal or cassava. I make pounded yam using an electric mixer by boiling the yam, then mixing it in a stand mixer before taking it out and kneading it with some extra water if needed. For rice dough, I cook the rice to two-thirds done, remove it from the heat, rinse it to remove the starch, then finish cooking it by adding a tiny bit of olive oil.

I don't use oil or fat when I cook meat. I cook the meat first and then use the juice that the meat releases to brown the onions and other ingredients. These are all little techniques and tips I learned from my mother.

> Buying good produce, good meat from a butcher, and good-quality fish from a fishmonger changes everything!

PLACALI
(cassava fufu)

DIFFICULTY: EASY · PREPARATION: 40 MINUTES + 1 HOUR RESTING TIME · COOKING: 15 MINUTES

**INGREDIENTS
FOR 6 PEOPLE**

1 lb 2 oz (500 g) placali
(fermented cassava paste)

PREPARATION

Put the placali in a bowl, add 2 cups (500 ml) water, and mix well.

Pour the mixture through a medium sieve twice to remove the fibers and any larger pieces.

Tilt the bowl with the placali in it by placing a small upturned plate underneath and leave the mixture to rest like this for 1 hour.

Use a ladle to carefully remove the white liquid on the surface of the mixture.

Place the placali in a pot and cook over low heat, stirring constantly with a wooden spoon. When the placali starts to cook (after around 2 minutes), vigorously stir with a wooden spoon, scraping the bottom and side of the pot until you get a smooth paste (this takes around 10 minutes).

To finish making the placali, wet your hands and use them to scrape the dough from the side of the pot and on the spoon, then put the dough into a large mortar or bowl to make balls.

Traditionally, placali is served in an oval-shaped ball, but you can also use a cookie or fondant cutter to give the fufu a more decorative shape and design.

CHEF ANTO'S TIP

Placali dough is a fermented cassava dough. It is also called "cassava fufu." You'll find frozen cassava paste or flour in some African or Asian grocery stores. The principle remains the same—you just need enough arm strength to constantly stir the dough without burning it. Cooking placali requires you to be present throughout the entire process. Innovate by adding spices or toasted nuts to boost flavor. Placali balls are served to accompany dishes with sauce.

EGGPLANTS WITH GUINEA SORREL

DIFFICULTY: EASY · PREPARATION: 30 MINUTES · COOKING: 1 HOUR 30 MINUTES

INGREDIENTS FOR 6 PEOPLE

1 lb 2 oz (500 g) African or other small eggplants

3½ oz (100 g) okra

1 bunch Guinea sorrel leaves (see tip)

3 tbsp green nokoss (see p. 26)

⅓ cup (90 ml) red palm oil

Salt and pepper

PREPARATION

Cook the eggplants in a pot of salted boiling water for 1 hour. Remove from the heat, drain, and leave to cool.

Carefully remove the eggplant stems and skin, then cut each one into quarters.

Cut the tops off the okra, then cut it in half lengthways.

Remove the sorrel stems, keeping only the leaves. Bunch the leaves together and finely chop them. Set aside.

In a frying pan, sweat the green nokoss in the red palm oil for 3 minutes. Add the okra and brown over medium heat for 10 minutes. Stir in the chopped sorrel and cook for 5 minutes. Add the eggplants, season with salt and pepper, and leave to simmer for 5 minutes.

CHEF ANTO'S TIP

Guinea sorrel leaves are also called hibiscus, roselle, or bissap leaves (the botanical name is Hibiscus sabdariffa). *Be careful not to confuse them with hibiscus or bissap flowers, which are red or white, depending on the variety, or with garden sorrel, which is another edible green. Look for Guinea sorrel leaves in African, Carribbean, or South Asian grocery stores, or substitute other spicy greens.*

There are several types of African eggplant: some are green (bitter) and some are white (sweet). This dish works with both types—it just depends on your taste preferences. It's a good side for fish and fried or roasted meats. To serve it as a main meal, add some smoked fish or sardines in oil.

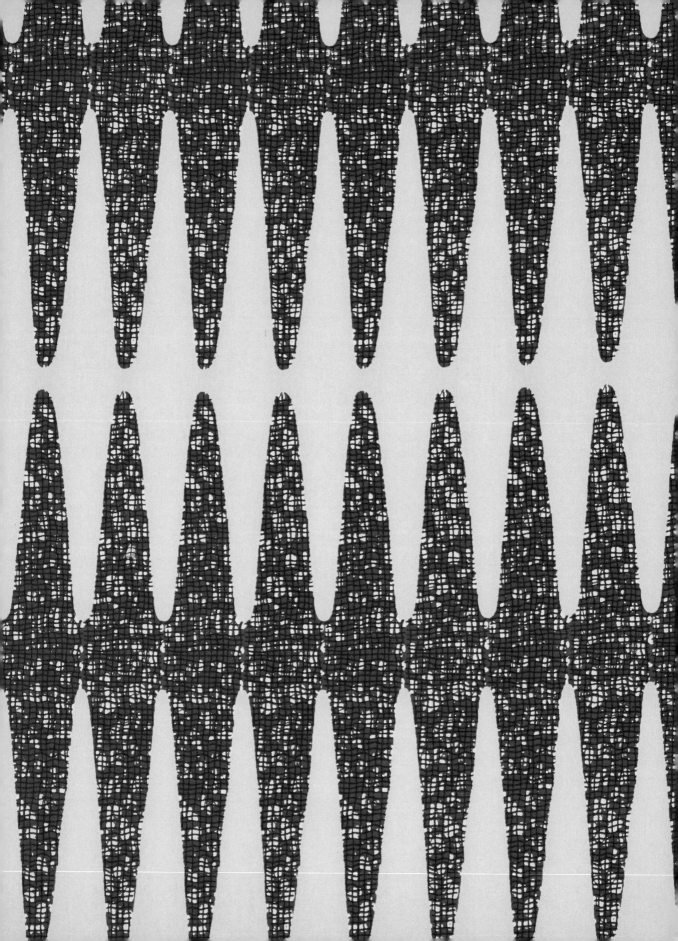

STREET FOOD

ITS EXOTIQ

L'AFRICA PARIS

BEEF BAGUETTE

DIFFICULTY: EASY • PREPARATION: 10 MINUTES • COOKING: 15 MINUTES

INGREDIENTS
FOR 6 PEOPLE

2 red onions

1 tomato

⅓ cup (85 g) homemade or good-quality mayonnaise

1 tsp ntorolo (see p. 27)

1 tbsp red nokoss (see p. 26)

Vegetable oil

9 oz (250 g) ground beef

Salt and pepper

3 small baguettes

A handful of lettuce leaves, to serve

PREPARATION

Peel and thinly slice the red onions. Cut the tomato in half and slice it into half-rounds.

Mix the mayonnaise and ntorolo together.

In a frying pan, sweat the red nokoss in a little oil, add the ground beef, and cook for 15 minutes. Season with salt and pepper. Set aside.

Cut the baguettes in half and then split them open. Spread the ntorolo mayonnaise over the baguettes. Add some lettuce and tomato and onion slices to each baguette, then add the ground beef and any juices. Serve immediately.

CHEF ANTO'S TIP

Beef baguette is an African street food invention. There is no set recipe. The idea is to make a baguette with roasted or grilled meat, fresh vegetables, mayonnaise, and chile.

FRIED SARDINES

DIFFICULTY: EASY • PREPARATION: 10 MINUTES • COOKING: 30 MINUTES

INGREDIENTS
FOR 6 PEOPLE

2 lb 4 oz (1 kg) fresh sardines

Salt

½ cup (60 g) all-purpose flour or fine cornmeal

Vegetable oil for deep-frying

Lemon wedges

PREPARATION

Carefully scale the sardines and then, keeping them whole, gut them through the head. Wash the sardines and pat dry.

Make diagonal cuts in the skin on both sides of each sardine, from the head to the tail.

Sprinkle the sardines with salt, then sprinkle them with flour.

Deep-fry the sardines in the hot oil until they are cooked through and the meat and bones are crunchy. Drain on paper towels.

Serve the sardines as a snack or as an appetizer, with lemon wedges for squeezing.

GRILLED FISH

DIFFICULTY: MEDIUM • PREPARATION: 15 MINUTES • COOKING: 30 MINUTES

INGREDIENTS
FOR 4 PEOPLE

4 sea bream

Scant ½ cup (100 ml) instant marinade (see p. 30)

Vegetable oil

PREPARATION

Scale the bream, then gut them through the head and rinse, keeping the fish whole. You can ask your fishmonger to do this if you like.

Cut off the fins and make three relatively deep cuts in the skin on both sides of each fish.

Using a pastry brush, brush the fish with the marinade, making sure that it fills the incisions, the head, and inside of the fish.

Prepare your barbecue. When the barbecue is hot, liberally brush the grill with vegetable oil to coat it completely.

Grill the fish, basting it with the marinade periodically, for 15 minutes on each side, or until cooked to your liking.

CHEF ANTO'S TIP
The cooking time will depend on the size of the fish. During cooking, continue to baste the fish with the marinade so it doesn't dry out. Once the fish is cooked, serve it with the remaining marinade, allokos (fried plantains, see p. 128), and cassava semolina. If you don't have a barbecue, you can make this recipe using a grill pan or your broiler.

Franco-Cameroonian visual pop artist Fred Ebami is taking digital art by storm, bringing an avant-garde and refreshingly new perspective to traditional pop art. His world is a combination of Basquiat, Andy Warhol, Lichtenstein, and Oliviero Toscani, making him a link between previous generations and those of today and tomorrow.

Fred Ebami works from photos and drawings that he reworks digitally using Photoshop. He creates visuals using different media (wood, canvas, paper, rhodoid plastic, and even using 3D printing) that he then colors using Posca® paint markers, spray paint, or paint. This technique gives him a unique connection between the organic and digital world. He plays with slogans to convey his vision of the world, images to carry a message, and bright colors to attract attention and awaken the senses. With his passion for posters and lithographs, Fred's works often resemble advertisements.

Fred Ebami's inventive and playful style sets him apart and is easily recognizable. It reflects his contemplative, direct, inquisitive, and communicative nature. He is a founding member of the On A Slamé Sur La Lune collective, an organization that promotes public education and raises awareness around cultural heritage and dialogue through cultural activities and events.

At age 40, Fred Ebami is regarded as one of the only African heritage pop artists known around the world. Appearing in the *French Black Gotha* and that of Europe, he was named one of the most influential African artists in 2018 by *Tropics* magazine in South Africa and is listed on Artsper and the auction house Hôtel des ventes de Monte-Carlo (presented by SEVEN GALLERY / Jacques DEVOS).

www.facebook.com/FredEbami
www.instagram.com/fredebami

What are your favorite Sub-Saharan African dishes? A star ingredient?

There are several, but it would be the food from Cameroon, where I come from. Even as a very young child I remember the smells coming from the kitchen when my mother was cooking.

There was a dish that we call "mbongo tchobi"; it's a black sauce made using a "burned seed," the mbongo seed (a kind of wild Cameroonian pepper) and fish (tjobl means "fish" in Bassa). It is a very typical dish of the Bassa people.

Otherwise it would have to be ndolé, our national dish and one that is now international, too. I love ndolé! Especially the one my mother makes. Each region has its own way of making this dish, but what I like about it is the mix of spices and ginger that makes it both bitter and sweet.

Then there are the other traditional dishes I remember all too well, like the really strong taste of the "yellow sauce" made from palm kernels, mixed with smoked fish and eaten with taro (or nsùgui, in Bassa). I love the pure yellow color, the smell of the fish stock, and the sweetness of the taro. The star ingredient for me would be chile. I love spicy food!

Does this trigger a taste memory, like Proust's madeleine?

My memories are mostly of street food, it's the thing that really transports me back to Cameroon, like puff-puff and beans that you could eat for breakfast, lunch, or dinner, whenever you wanted! When I eat them it always brings back memories. When I met Marc Alexandre (Captain Alexandre) on the soccer field in Cameroon as a pre-teen, we would go and eat puff-puff and beans after each match. It's a bit like going to McDonald's (but better!). It's the thing that's there, it doesn't change, never goes out of fashion, and it's always good! It's a convivial dish—you get together in the street around the big pots where the women fry the puff-puff and it's a chance to take a bit of time out and relax. The first time I met Marc on the soccer field, we became friends, and afterwards we asked each other: "What do we do now? Well, how about going to eat puff-puff?" (*Laughs.*) After that it became our ritual, and each time we met or came home from school, that was what we'd do: "Meet you at the puff-puff stall?!"

Even now that we are adults, when we meet at each other's houses, there is always puff-puff and beans—other dishes as well, but always puff-puff and beans on the side.

Other than that, I like anything that's grilled—fish, chicken, or suya (meat cooked over coals). These dishes always transport me back to my country. Whether I am in England or the United States, if I eat these dishes I feel like I am back in my homeland.

What is your connection to this cuisine now?

There is still a very strong connection for me. Even now, I have to eat at my mother's place at least once a week, for example. These comforting meals are linked to many family memories. It's also the special taste of a mother's dish that is never the same if it is made by someone else!

I am strongly attached to this cuisine, but I often try to reinvent these dishes with other ingredients that are not necessarily traditional. For example, to have a bit of fun, I might make peanut sauce with dried meat or fried fish, which is not usually done. I have kept the traditional connection to the basic recipe, but I will add my own little bit of creativity—something a bit different, my own personal touch.

Do you have a tip, a short recipe, or any cooking advice?

Don't stop the first time a dish is a "flop"—keep going, and don't be scared of being inventive. Then, when you have mastered a dish, try changing things up a bit, the flavors or spices, use different condiments or other types of meat or fish. I love being inventive, shaking up tradition a bit! I see cooking as a game, you have to have fun! Just like when you paint, you create ... and then you observe, it can be something amazing, or perhaps not so amazing, but you might just be surprised. I think that must be how "fusion" restaurants came about—they combined ingredients that were normally not used together and it ended up being delicious. But the most important thing is to have fun!

> I see cooking as a game, you have to have fun! Like when you paint, you create ...

BANANA FRITTERS

DIFFICULTY: EASY • PREPARATION: 20 MINUTES + 1 HOUR RESTING TIME • COOKING: 30 MINUTES

INGREDIENTS FOR 25–30 FRITTERS

6 very ripe bananas

½ cup (60 g) all-purpose flour

Scant ½ cup (60 g) fine cornmeal

1 pinch salt

¼ cup (60 ml) lukewarm milk

⅛ oz (6 g) fresh yeast, or ⅔ tsp (2 g) instant yeast

Vegetable oil for deep-frying

Confectioners' sugar, vanilla ice cream, or melted chocolate, to serve (optional)

PREPARATION

Peel and cut the bananas into pieces. Place them in a bowl and mash using a fork or rolling pin.

Add the flour, cornmeal, and salt and mix until combined.

Mix the warmed milk and yeast in a bowl. Mix the yeast mixture into the banana mixture. Cover the bowl and leave the dough to rise in a warm place for 1 hour.

Knock down the dough to remove the gas formed by the yeast.

In a deep-fryer or deep heavy-based pot, heat the oil to 340–350°F (170–180°C). Using a spoon, make balls of dough and drop them into the hot oil. Cook in batches until golden all over. Drain the fritters on paper towels.

Serve the fritters hot, dusted with confectioners' sugar, alongside vanilla ice cream, or drizzled with melted chocolate, or eat them plain alongside spicy sauce dishes.

CHEF ANTO'S TIP

These fritters can be eaten as a sweet snack dusted with confectioners' sugar or with vanilla ice cream or melted chocolate, or as a savory snack with spicy sauce. You can use overripe regular bananas as well as overripe plantains. It's important to maintain the oil temperature between 340°F and 355°F (170°C and 180°C) so the fritters don't absorb too much oil.

CHINCHINS

INGREDIENTS FOR 2 LB 4 OZ (1 KG) CROQUETTES

4 cups (500 g) all-purpose flour, plus extra if needed

⅔ cup (150 g) superfine or regular sugar

½ tsp ground cinnamon

2 pinches salt

1 vanilla bean

14 tbsp (200 g) softened butter or margarine

3 eggs

4 tsp milk

4 cups (1 liter) vegetable oil, for deep-frying

PREPARATION

In a large bowl, mix the flour, sugar, cinnamon, and salt. Split the vanilla bean lengthways and scrape the seeds into the bowl.

Add the softened butter and mix until combined. Add the eggs and continue to knead together.

Add the milk and mix until you have a dough that is not too sticky, adding a little extra flour if necessary. Leave to rest in the fridge for 1 hour.

Roll out the dough on a board, then use a knife to cut the dough into small squares. Form the croquettes into your desired shape.

Heat the oil in a pot and fry the croquettes in batches until golden, moving them around to make sure they don't stick together.

When the chinchins are golden, remove and drain on paper towels to absorb the excess oil. Leave to cool before serving.

CHEF ANTO'S TIP

You can vary this sweet recipe by flavoring your dough with citrus zest or adding cocoa powder to the flour. The chinchins will keep well in an airtight container in a dry place away from any moisture.

CASHEW NOUGAT

DIFFICULTY: EASY • PREPARATION: 5 MINUTES • COOKING: 10 MINUTES

INGREDIENTS FOR AROUND 20 PIECES OF NOUGAT

Vegetable oil

1¾ cups (200 g) unsalted cashews

⅔ cup (150 g) sugar

⅓ cup (100 g) raw honey

1 pinch salt

PREPARATION

Oil a cutting board and set aside.

Roughly crush the cashews by hand or using a food processor.

Melt the sugar in a pot over medium heat until it caramelizes, then add the honey, salt, and cashews and mix well.

From this step on, you need to work fast so that the mixture doesn't harden too quickly! Pour the mixture onto the oiled board and flatten it using a rolling pin until it's around ½ inch (1 cm) thick.

Cut the mixture into squares while it's still hot.

CHEF ANTO'S TIP

Called "kongodo" in Equatorial Guinea, or "nkate cake" in Ghana, this nut brittle–like sweet is also found in the Comores (chihondro), in West Africa ("bonbons caramel"), in Mozambique ("matortore"), and even in the Antilles, where it is known as "nougat antillais" or "sik à pistaches," depending on the region.

If you don't have cashews, use peanuts, almonds, coconut flakes, or toasted African pistachios (see tip p. 116).

CRISPY DOUGHNUT BALLS

DIFFICULTY: EASY • PREPARATION: 5 MINUTES + 30 MINUTES RESTING TIME • COOKING: 10 MINUTES

INGREDIENTS FOR AROUND 20 DOUGHNUT BALLS

2 eggs

⅓ cup (75 g) sugar

Scant ½ cup (100 ml) full-fat evaporated milk

2½ tbsp red palm oil

2 tsp orange flower water

1 pinch salt

1½ cups (250 g) fine cornmeal

4 tsp baking powder

Vegetable oil for deep-frying

PREPARATION

Break the eggs into a bowl, add the sugar, and whisk until the mixture turns white and frothy. Add the evaporated milk, red palm oil, orange flower water, and salt, then whisk until the mixture is smooth.

Add the cornmeal and baking powder, then use your hands to knead the mixture into a sticky dough. Set the dough aside for 30 minutes.

In a large pot, heat enough oil for deep-frying. Once the oil is hot, dip your hand in water before forming balls of dough using your thumb, index finger, and middle finger. Drop the balls into the oil and fry until evenly golden.

Drain on paper towels before serving the doughnut balls warm.

GOMBO
CÔTE D'IVOIRE

PE Petites   IES
C AUBERGINES =

DESSERTS

PEANUT FINANCIERS

DIFFICULTY: EASY • PREPARATION: 20 MINUTES • COOKING: 15 MINUTES

INGREDIENTS FOR AROUND 20 FINANCIERS

⅔ cup (100 g) roasted unsalted peanuts

14 tbsp (200 g) butter, plus extra for greasing

2 tbsp peanut butter

6 egg whites

1¾ cups (200 g) confectioners' sugar, plus extra for dusting

⅔ cup (80 g) all-purpose flour

1 tbsp crushed roasted peanuts

PREPARATION

Preheat the oven to 350°F (180°C). Grease a financier pan or mini muffin pan.

In a food processor, pulse the roasted peanuts to a fine powder.

Melt the butter in a small pot and cook until it is lightly browned but not burned. Add the peanut butter and leave to cool.

Beat the egg whites and confectioners' sugar in a bowl until firm peaks form. Gently add the flour, a little at a time, then add the peanut powder and the butter mixture. Gently fold together, being careful not to deflate the egg whites.

Spoon the batter into the pan and sprinkle the tops with the crushed peanuts. Place in the oven and bake for 15 minutes.

Serve the financiers warm, dusted with confectioners' sugar.

MANGO TART

DIFFICULTY: MEDIUM • PREPARATION: 1 HOUR + FREEZING AND RESTING TIME • COOKING: 1 HOUR

INGREDIENTS
FOR 6 PEOPLE

4 very ripe Kent mangoes

1 lime

4 tbsp (60 g) unsalted butter

⅓ cup (100 g) raw honey

4 gelatin leaves, or 2 tsp unflavored gelatin powder

⅓ cup (90 ml) light cream

1 cup (200 g) granulated sugar

FOR THE WHITE CHOCOLATE CREAM

½ cup (120 ml) heavy whipping cream

½ vanilla bean

3½ oz (100 g) white chocolate

FOR THE COOKIE BASE

1½ cups (190 g) all-purpose flour

⅔ cup (60 g) ground African pistachios (see tip p. 116) or raw pumpkin seeds

1 cup (125 g) confectioners' sugar

1 pinch salt

1 stick plus 1 tbsp (125 g) butter, cubed

1 egg

PREPARATION

Peel the mangoes and cut the flesh into small cubes. Zest the lime. Melt the butter and honey in a frying pan, then add the mango cubes and stir to coat well. Add the lime zest (reserving a little for the garnish) and cook for around 10 minutes—the mangoes must be very soft—then set aside.

Place the gelatin in a bowl of 2 tbsp cold water to dissolve. Heat the cream in a small pot over low heat. Pour the sugar into a heavy-based saucepan and cook over medium heat until caramelized. Immediately remove from the heat and carefully add the hot cream, stirring well. Add the gelatin (squeezed out if using leaves) and mix well until dissolved. Stir in the mango mixture, then pour the filling into an 8 inch (20 cm) round silicone mold or cake pan. Leave to cool to room temperature, then place in the freezer for at least 3 hours.

For the white chocolate cream, pour the cream into a small pot, then split the vanilla bean in half and scrape the seeds into the cream. Bring to a boil, then remove from the heat, add the white chocolate, and stir until it is completely melted. Leave to cool to room temperature, then place in the freezer for 30 minutes. Whip the cream using an electric mixer and set aside in the fridge.

For the base, preheat the oven to 350°F (180°C). Sift the flour, African pistachios, confectioners' sugar, and salt together, then add the butter, a little at a time. Work the mixture between your fingers until it resembles breadcrumbs. Make a well in this mixture and break the egg into the center. Knead together using your hands until you have a smooth ball of dough, then wrap well and place in the fridge to rest for 30 minutes.

Roll out the dough on a sheet of parchment paper to a circle at least 1¼ inches (3 cm) larger than the diameter of your silicone mold. Prick the dough with a fork and return it to the fridge for at least 30 minutes, then place on a baking pan and bake for 30 minutes. Set aside to cool.

Turn the frozen mango filling out onto the cookie base and set aside for 1–2 hours for the filling to defrost. Pipe or dollop the white chocolate cream around the edge and sprinkle with lime zest.

BAOBAB CRÈME BRÛLÉE

DIFFICULTY: EASY • PREPARATION: 20 MINUTES + 5 HOURS CHILLING TIME • COOKING: 40 MINUTES

INGREDIENTS
FOR 6 PEOPLE

1 vanilla bean

2 cups (500 ml) light cream

6 egg yolks

¼ cup (50 g) sugar

1 tbsp baobab powder (see tip)

Scant ½ cup (90 g) light brown sugar

PREPARATION

Preheat the oven to 320°F (160°C).

Split the vanilla bean in half lengthways and scrape out the seeds. Pour the cream into a pot, add the empty vanilla bean, and cook over low heat until simmering. Turn off the heat and leave to infuse for 5 minutes.

Beat the egg yolks, sugar, and vanilla seeds together until frothy. Discard the vanilla bean, then slowly pour the cream into the egg yolk mixture. Mix well, add the baobab powder, and mix again.

Pour the cream mixture into 6 ramekins, then place them in a bain-marie (a deep roasting pan filled with enough boiling water to reach halfway up the sides of the ramekins). Bake for 30–35 minutes until the custard is set but wobbly like a flan.

Leave the custards to cool at room temperature for 1 hour, then place them in the fridge for at least 4 hours.

Before serving, sprinkle a layer of light brown sugar on top of the ramekins and caramelize it under the broiler or using a culinary blow torch.

CHEF ANTO'S TIP

Baobab powder comes from the fruit of the baobab tree, and is very high in vitamin C. It can be found at most health food stores.

MBOURAKÉ

DIFFICULTY: EASY · PREPARATION: 20 MINUTES · COOKING: NONE

INGREDIENTS
FOR 4 PEOPLE

1 lb 2 oz (500 g) stale bread

2¼ tbsp light brown sugar

¼ cup (70 g) peanut butter

Scant ½ cup (100 ml) evaporated milk

PREPARATION

In a large mortar, crush the bread until it becomes a powder. Add the brown sugar and continue to crush and mix well. Tip the bread mixture into a bowl, mix in the peanut butter, and work the dough with your hands until it is crumbly.

Gradually add the evaporated milk, continuing to work the mbouraké with your hands to make it crumbly.

Serve with stewed fruit, ice cream, or yogurt.

CHEF ANTO'S TIP

From the Wolof word "mburaake," which means "dry couscous or breadcrumbs," mbouraké is a Senegalese dessert that is traditionally made with crushed millet, peanut butter, and sugar. In the cities, millet has been replaced by stale bread. To save time, you can also replace the stale bread with dried breadcrumbs.

THIAKRY WITH STRAWBERRY COULIS

DIFFICULTY: EASY · PREPARATION : 15 MINUTES + 2 HOURS CHILLING · COOKING: 10 MINUTES

INGREDIENTS
FOR 6 PEOPLE

Scant 1 cup (200 ml) milk

1 vanilla bean

½ cup (50 g) millet

1 egg

2¼ tbsp light brown sugar

5½ oz (150 g) cream cheese

¼ cup (50 g) crème fraîche

A few strawberries, sliced

FOR THE COULIS

9 oz (250 g) strawberries, hulled

¼ cup (55 g) sugar

Juice of ½ lemon

Scant ½ cup (100 ml) bissap (see p. 192)

PREPARATION

Pour the milk into a pot. Split the vanilla bean in half lengthways and scrape the seeds into the pot. Add the empty bean and bring the milk to a boil. Stir in the millet, then turn off the heat, cover, and set aside for 10 minutes. Discard the vanilla bean. Fluff the millet with a fork, and leave to cool.

Using a hand mixer or whisk, beat the egg with the brown sugar until frothy. Add the cream cheese and the crème fraîche, then whisk until smooth. Whisk in the millet, a little at a time. Pour the mixture into glass pots or ramekins and leave to set in the fridge for at least 2 hours.

To prepare the coulis, put the strawberries, sugar, and lemon juice in a blender. Blend until smooth, then gradually blend in the bissap. Pour the coulis through a sieve to remove the seeds.

Serve the thiakry with the strawberry coulis and strawberry slices.

CHEF ANTO'S TIP

Strawberries in Africa? Yes! Contrary to common preconceptions, strawberries are not only grown in temperate countries. This means that you can find red fruits such as strawberries and cherries in Cameroon, Gabon, Guinea, Burkina Faso, Senegal, and the Ivory Coast.

Thiakry, or déguê, is very popular in West Africa, especially in regions where millet is commonly eaten. It's a favorite among children for breakfast or as a dessert.

Aïssé N'Diaye is the creator of the brand Afrikanista, a clothing collection that pays tribute to former African generations and the Sub-Saharan culture in West Africa in particular. The brand is structured around four themes: vintage photos of African families, African quotes and slogans, Egyptian hieroglyphs, and the "Funky Diva" spirit—through the shoulder pads found on some of the T-shirts and sweatshirts, which represent a woman who is confident in herself and in her style, who is both independent and bold.

The Afrikanista concept is based on handing down knowledge and tradition. And when it comes to what inspired Aïssé N'Diaye to become an entrepreneur, she quotes Marcus Garvey: "Ambition is the desire to progress and improve your circumstances ... It's wanting what is worth it and fighting to get it. Moving forward without looking back until you have achieved your goal."

Aïssé N'Diaye also finds inspiration in art, literature, and the history of Ancient Egypt, all of which she has been passionate about since she was a child.

After a long period of reflection, she has come to see the creation of Afrikanista as the culmination of her own personality: "I have always asked myself questions about my status as a black African woman. It all started with letting my hair return to its natural state, boosting my self-esteem and researching my family history and background. I asked my parents and relatives a lot of questions about our family tree, but also about their life, experiences, and arrival in France."

Aïssé N'Diaye seeks to convey an image that is unique to herself: "The message I'd like to communicate through the brand is an attachment to our roots, respect for our parents, and the richness of African culture through the Egyptian hieroglyphs and African proverbs."

www.afrikanista.com

It's not just about T-shirts and fashion. The clothing becomes a universal symbol across cultures: it brings together style and history. In this way, the brand allows even the least experienced to gain a greater understanding of the work of photographer Seydou Keïta, and to explore African proverbs and ancient Egyptian hieroglyphs.

What are your favorite Sub-Saharan African dishes? A star ingredient?
My favorite dishes in this cuisine are soupou kandja, déré, and mollé. Soupou kandja is a white rice-based dish, with an okra and palm oil sauce. This is a dish that is particularly special to me; it is mainly cooked in Senegal and Mauritania. Déré is typically from Mauritania. It has wheat or corn coucous (or millet) and a sauce made with spinach leaves and pounded peanuts. It is also a dish that I really enjoy. Mollé is a variation of déré—it's also a wheat or corn couscous dish, but is served with a peanut butter and black-eyed pea sauce. Both déré and mollé are cooked with meat. We usually use mutton, but they can be made with beef as well.

My star ingredient is dakatine, or peanut butter. We prepare many dishes with dakatine, using processed or pounded peanuts. We buy a lot of peanuts. In Mauritania, in the village where my parents come from, there are a lot of peanut plantations, so there are many recipes using this ingredient.

Does this trigger a taste memory, like Proust's madeleine?

In relation to déré and mollé, one of my earliest memories is of my father buying a sheep every month to feed our large family. Either on the day the sheep was bought or the day after, my mother would prepare either fouto mollé or fouto déré. The whole process was all a bit ceremonial because preparing the couscous itself takes a long time—you have to steam it several times in a couscoussier. Then, the couscous needs to be colored with a green plant-derived powder called mouloukhia. And then you have to make the sauce separately. In any event, these two dishes take a huge amount of time to make.

My father would invite his friends and family to enjoy the meal together. For me, these dishes always represent a day of celebration, with many people joining us at home, including our whole family and lots of children.

Soupou kandja (okra and palm oil sauce) is also a childhood dish for me. I first ate this dish when I was invited to a Gambian friend's house as a child. Her mother made it with green peas and I really liked it, so when I went home I asked my mother: "Why don't you put green peas in the soupou kandja?" She replied that people in Gambia usually make it that way, with green peas and also adding shrimp with the meat, whereas she normally cooked traditional Mauritanian food.

The region where my parents are from is very close to Senegal—it's only the Senegal River that separates us. That means that there are quite a number of Senegalese dishes like yassa and thiep (thiep bou dien) with several variations: thiep bou dien with red rice and fish, and thiep yap with meat like chicken, mutton, or oxtail. Oxtail thiep is also something I really enjoy. It's really good, the meat is so tender, it's a real pleasure to eat. (*Laughs.*)

> I always buy chiles and a can of dakatine, plantains ... the basics!

What is your connection to this cuisine now?

I do cook, even though I don't have much time outside of work. I like cooking and I like having all the ingredients on hand ready to cook. To make sure I have everything I need, I go to Château Rouge (an African quarter in Paris) to buy supplies, including okra—even if I don't have time to cook them straight away, they are cut up and kept in freezer bags for when I want to make mafé or okra sauce.

I always buy chiles and a can of dakatine, plantains ... the basics! I really love fried plantains (allokos, p. 128)—they're delicious!

Otherwise, I go to my mother's place very often, at least once every couple of weeks, so I eat "local" food there. Last weekend, my mother prepared a drink that I had never tasted, made from milk, monkey bread (the fruit of the baobab tree), pineapple, and peach. It was very refreshing!

Do you have a tip, a short recipe, or any cooking advice?

My tip would be for cooking rice. I don't use a rice cooker, I make it in the traditional way. I bring water to a boil and add the quantity of rice needed. Once the rice is added, I remove the excess water, add a little bit of sunflower or olive oil, and once the rice has absorbed most of the water, I cover it tightly with foil and lower the temperature as much as possible to leave the rice to cook properly, without scorching it. I prefer to cook it like this—it's not dry and not too soft, either. Let's say it's al dente rice! (*Laughs.*)

COCONUT RICE WITH FRUIT TARTARE

DIFFICULTY: EASY · PREPARATION: 30 MINUTES · COOKING: 45 MINUTES

INGREDIENTS
FOR 6 PEOPLE

7 oz (200 g) speculoos cookies (Dutch spiced cookies)

5 tbsp (80 g) unsalted softened butter

2 cups (500 ml) coconut milk

½ cup (100 g) parboiled long-grain rice

5 tbsp sugar

1 vanilla bean

1½ oz (40 g) white chocolate

¼ pomegranate

½ mango

¼ pineapple

Thinly sliced zest of 1 lime

Small edible flowers, such as cilantro flowers or pansies

PREPARATION

Crush the speculoos cookies in a bowl, add the softened butter, and mix well. Press the cookie mixture into round tart rings to make the bases. Set aside.

Combine half the coconut milk in a pot with the rice and sugar. Split the vanilla bean lengthways and scrape the seeds into the pot, then add the empty bean. Bring to a boil, then reduce the heat to low and cook, stirring constantly, until the rice has absorbed all of the coconut milk. Gradually add the remaining coconut milk and cook until the grains of rice are mushy.

Add the white chocolate to the hot rice and stir until it is completely melted. Remove the vanilla bean and leave to cool.

Remove the seeds from the pomegranate. Peel and dice the mango and pineapple. Put the pomegranate seeds and diced fruit into a bowl, add the lime zest (reserving some to garnish), and mix together.

Assemble the dessert like a cheesecake by topping the cookie bases with the cold coconut rice. Decorate with the diced fruit, lime zest, and a few edible flowers. Serve chilled.

CHEF ANTO'S TIP

Rice with milk is called "sombi" in Senegal and Mali. It can be made with corn. You can also flambé the diced fruit with rum or other alcohol, or marinate it with cinnamon, star anise, or other spices. This dessert can also be served with a fruit coulis or a caramel or chocolate sauce.

EVAPORATED MILK AND LIME ICE CREAM

DIFFICULTY: EASY • PREPARATION: 25 MINUTES + 3 HOURS FREEZING TIME • COOKING: NONE

INGREDIENTS
FOR 6 PEOPLE

6 large limes

⅔ cup (150 g) sugar

1½ tsp vanilla sugar

3¼ cups (820 g) canned evaporated milk

Toasted coconut flakes

PREPARATION

Wash, zest, and juice the limes.

Combine the sugar, vanilla sugar, and lime juice in a bowl and stir until the sugar has dissolved. Add the evaporated milk.

Beat the mixture with an electric mixer for 20 minutes (it will become a creamy mousse). Mix in the lime zest.

Pour the mixture into an ice-cream maker or container and freeze for at least 3 hours.

Serve the ice cream in bowls, decorated with some toasted coconut.

CHEF ANTO'S TIP

For the best results, churn the lime mousse in an ice-cream maker before freezing. This will give the ice cream an even creamier taste. If you don't have vanilla sugar, use 1 tsp vanilla extract and 1 tsp sugar.

SORGHUM CUPCAKES WITH WHIPPED GANACHE

DIFFICULTY: EASY · PREPARATION: 25 MINUTES + 1 HOUR FREEZING TIME · COOKING: 15 MINUTES

INGREDIENTS FOR 12 CUPCAKES

2 eggs

½ cup (100 g) sugar

7 tbsp (100 g) melted butter

1 tsp vanilla extract

¼ tsp ground cinnamon

¾ cup (100 g) sorghum flour

½ tsp baking soda

Crushed roasted peanuts, to decorate

FOR THE WHIPPED GANACHE

Scant 1 cup (200 ml) heavy whipping cream

3½ oz (100 g) white chocolate

PREPARATION

Preheat the oven to 300°F (150°C). Line a cupcake pan with paper baking cups.

Beat the eggs with the sugar until pale. Mix in the melted butter, vanilla, and cinnamon. Mix in the sorghum flour and baking soda.

Half-fill the cupcake papers with the batter. Bake for 15 minutes or until golden. Set aside to cool.

For the whipped ganache, heat the cream until almost boiling, then remove from the heat. Add the white chocolate and stir until completely melted. Leave to cool to room temperature, then place in the freezer for 1 hour.

Whip the chilled ganache using an electric mixer.

Frost the cupcakes with the whipped ganache and sprinkle with the crushed peanuts.

CHEF ANTO'S TIP

Sorghum is a grain that is rich in fiber and protein. It is a smart food—it's good for consumers because of its nutritional qualities, good for producers due to its high yield, and good for the planet as it doesn't require much water to grow.

SPICED PINEAPPLE WITH CASSAVA CRUMBLE

DIFFICULTY: EASY • PREPARATION: 30 MINUTES • COOKING: 1 HOUR 15 MINUTES

INGREDIENTS
FOR 4 PEOPLE

1 small pineapple

FOR THE CARAMEL

1 inch (2.5 cm) piece ginger

1 vanilla bean

½ cup (100 g) sugar

3½ tbsp (50 g) butter

½ tsp ground cinnamon

2 star anise

4 tsp gold rum

Scant ½ cup (100 ml) pineapple juice

FOR THE CRUMBLE

⅓ cups (50 g) garri (fermented, dried, and ground cassava)

Scant ½ cup (50 g) all-purpose flour

½ cup (50 g) ground African pistachios (see tip p. 116) or raw pumpkin seeds

3½ tbsp (50 g) softened butter

¼ cup (50 g) light brown sugar

PREPARATION

Peel the pineapple and cut it into quarters, lengthwise, without removing the core.

For the caramel, peel the ginger and cut it into thin strips. Split the vanilla bean in half lengthways and scrape out the seeds.

Pour the sugar into a heavy-based pot and cook over medium heat until caramelized. Carefully add the butter and stir to combine, then remove from the heat. Add the cinnamon, ginger strips, star anise, and the vanilla bean and seeds, then mix again. Add the pineapple pieces and cook for 10 minutes on each side.

Deglaze the caramel with the rum and flambé it (carefully light it on fire), then pour in the pineapple juice. Cook over low heat, turning the pineapple pieces regularly, for 45 minutes.

Preheat the oven to 350°F (180°C). Line a baking pan with parchment paper.

To make the crumble, mix all the ingredients together in a bowl, spread the mixture on the lined baking pan, and bake for 15 minutes. Leave to cool and set aside.

Sprinkle the crumble on plates, then place a piece of warm pineapple on top of each, and drizzle with the caramel.

POIRES BELLE HAWA
(poached pears with chocolate sauce)

DIFFICULTY: EASY · PREPARATION: 30 MINUTES · COOKING: 45 MINUTES

**INGREDIENTS
FOR 6 PEOPLE**

6 pears

4 cups (1 liter) bissap
(see p. 192)

1¼ cups (250 g) sugar

2 small vanilla beans

2 cloves

2¼ cups (250 g) roasted
cashews

Dark chocolate shavings,
to serve

FOR THE WHIPPED CREAM

2 cups (500 ml) heavy
whipping cream

¼ cup (50 g) confectioners'
sugar

FOR THE CHOCOLATE SAUCE

Scant 1 cup (200 ml) light
cream

Scant 1 cup (200 ml) lowfat
milk

7 oz (200 g) 64% dark
chocolate, broken into
pieces

PREPARATION

Peel the pears, keeping the stems intact. Push an apple corer into each pear from the base to remove around 2 inches (5 cm) of the core and seeds. Cut the bases of the pears so that they will stand upright.

Combine the bissap, sugar, vanilla, and cloves in a pot and bring to a boil. Add the pears and cook over low heat for 25 minutes (check if they are done using the tip of a small knife, which should pierce the fruit easily). Remove the pot from the heat and leave to cool to room temperature.

Remove the pears from the pot and strain the juice. Return the juice to the heat and cook until it is reduced and syrupy. Dip the pears halfway into the syrup, then leave them to drain on a wire rack.

To prepare the whipped cream, whisk the cream with a mixer or by hand, gradually adding the confectioners' sugar, until stiff peaks form. Keep well chilled.

To prepare the chocolate sauce, bring the cream and milk to a boil, tip in the chocolate pieces, then mix until the sauce is smooth.

Roughly chop the cashews and put them in a bowl. Dip the lower half of each pear into the chocolate, then into the crushed cashews.

To serve, spoon some chocolate sauce in the center of each plate and place a pear on top. Using two dessert spoons, make a rounded dollop of whipped cream and sprinkle it with dark chocolate shavings.

DRINKS

GNAMAKOUDJI
(ginger juice)

DIFFICULTY: EASY • PREPARATION: 20 MINUTES • COOKING: NONE

INGREDIENTS FOR 12 CUPS (3 LITERS)

2 lb 4 oz (1 kg) fresh ginger

3 limes

2 vanilla beans

1 cup (200 g) light brown sugar, packed

1 cinnamon stick

PREPARATION

Wash the ginger well and cut it into pieces. Using a juicer or extractor, extract the ginger juice.

Zest and juice the limes.

Split the vanilla beans in half lengthways and scrape out the seeds.

Add the brown sugar, vanilla beans and seeds, cinnamon stick, lime zest and juice, and ginger juice to a large jug. Mix well to dissolve the sugar, then add 10 cups (2.5 liters) water.

Keep in the fridge and serve chilled.

CHEF ANTO'S TIP

To vary the taste, you can replace the water with fruit juice (pineapple, mango, passionfruit, etc.). If you don't have a juicer, you can use unsweetened ginger juice.

Enjoyed as a mocktail or cocktail, gnamakoudji will make everyone happy. This drink also has therapeutic properties, such as soothing nausea in pregnant women and acting as an anti-inflammatory for coughs or bronchitis; it can be consumed either hot or cold. Gnamakoudji can be kept in the fridge for a week.

BISSAP

DIFFICULTY: EASY
PREPARATION: 20 MINUTES
COOKING: 15 MINUTES

INGREDIENTS FOR 4 PEOPLE

1¼ cups (50 g) dried bissap (hibiscus) flowers

⅔ cup (150 g) sugar

1 cinnamon stick

1 vanilla bean

1 bunch mint

PREPARATION

Bring 4 cups (1 liter) water to a boil. Add the bissap flowers, sugar, and cinnamon stick. Split the vanilla bean in half lengthways and scrape the seeds into the pot. Add the empty vanilla bean and cook for 15 minutes. Turn off the heat and add the mint. Cover and leave to infuse for 10 minutes.

Strain the mixture through a fine sieve and pour the infusion into a jug. Keep the bissap in the fridge for a week. Serve chilled.

BISSAPOLITAN

DIFFICULTY: EASY
PREPARATION: 10 MINUTES
COOKING: NONE

INGREDIENTS FOR 4 PEOPLE

Ice cubes

5¼ fl oz (160 ml) standard Russian vodka

5¼ fl oz (160 ml) Grand Marnier®

3½ fl oz (100 ml) bissap (see left)

1¼ fl oz (40 ml) lime juice

Lime slices, to serve

PREPARATION

In a shaker filled with ice cubes, vigorously shake all the ingredients together.

Pour into a cocktail glass, garnish with a slice of lime, and enjoy (in moderation!).

CHEF ANTO'S TIP

Better known as "hibiscus" in Europe and North America, "carcadé" in North Africa, "groseille-pays" in the Antilles, "sorel" or "flor of Jamaica" in the Caribbean, "fleur d'oseille" in Central Africa, or "bissap" in West Africa, this is the flower of the Guinea sorrel plant (its botanical name is Hibiscus sabdariffa). Its infusion is rich in vitamin C and trace minerals, and is also a good source of energy.

LA DIFFERENCE

BΛƷΛ MILKSHAKƎ
(baobab and banana)

DIFFICULTY: EASY · PREPARATION: 15 MINUTES · COOKING: NONE

INGREDIENTS
FOR 4 PEOPLE

2 overripe bananas

4 ice cubes

1 vanilla bean

**2 tbsp baobab powder
(see tip p. 170)**

2 tbsp light brown sugar

2 cups (500 ml) milk

PREPARATION

Put the bananas and ice cubes in a blender and blend for 1 minute.

Split the vanilla bean in half lengthways and scrape the seeds into the blender. Add the baobab powder, brown sugar, and half of the milk, then blend again for 1 minute.

Add the remaining milk and blend for another 1 minute or until frothy. Serve immediately.

KINKELIBA ICED TEA

DIFFICULTY: EASY · PREPARATION: 10 MINUTES · COOKING: 4 MINUTES

INGREDIENTS
FOR 4 PEOPLE

2 limes

½ cup (100 g) light brown sugar

¾ oz (20 g) dried kinkeliba leaves (see tip)

3 cardamom pods

1 cinnamon stick

Ice cubes

PREPARATION

Wash, zest, and juice the limes.

Bring 4 cups (1 liter) water to a boil in a pot, then add the lime zest, lime juice, and brown sugar.

Remove the pot from the heat, add the kinkeliba leaves, and infuse for 4 minutes. Strain, then add the cardamom pods and cinnamon stick and leave to cool.

Strain the cooled tea into glasses and serve with ice.

CHEF ANTO'S TIP

This refreshing iced tea is a great thirst-quencher. Kinkeliba leaves are used in traditional African medicine and are consumed to treat constipation and gallstones, and their anti-inflammatory and anti-microbial properties are used to soothe gastroenteritis. This tea will keep in the fridge for a week.

GINGER-CITRONELLA LEMONADE

DIFFICULTY: EASY · PREPARATION: 20 MINUTES · COOKING: 10 MINUTES

INGREDIENTS
FOR 4 PEOPLE

3 limes

1¾ oz (50 g) fresh ginger

3 fresh citronella stems

½ cup (130 g) light brown sugar

½ bunch peppermint

3 cups (750 ml) sparkling water

Lime and ginger slices, to serve

PREPARATION

Wash, zest, and juice the limes. Peel and finely grate the ginger. Cut the citronella into lengths of around 2 inches (5 cm).

Bring 1 cup (250 ml) of water to a boil in a pot. Add the lime zest, lime juice, citronella pieces, grated ginger, and brown sugar and mix well. When the sugar has completely dissolved, remove from the heat, add the peppermint, and leave to infuse for 4 minutes.

Strain the ginger mixture and dilute it with the sparkling water.

Serve chilled, with lime and ginger slices.

INDEX

BARBES, BELLEVILLE,
CHATEAU ROUGE,
DAKATINE, PLACE DE CLICHY

ACKNOWLEDGMENTS

MANGO

....

The publisher thanks Sonna International for their magnificent wax fabrics (front cover and chapter opening pages p. 24, 68, 126, 142, 164, and 188).

A big thank you in particular to David Cognon.

ALINE PRINCET

....

I would like to thank:

Chef Anto, who agreed to give us her excellent recipes and share her expert techniques and wisdom. She was instrumental to the project. The added bonus is that she is really photogenic, so her silhouette and her presence in some of the photos added glamor to this book! Thank you, Anto!

Séverine Charrier, who did the initial mock-up of this beautiful book and agreed to prepare a draft for me to present the project to publishers and show them the artistic approach I had in mind. Bravo! It is superb!

Francis Beugré, Cécile Bardin, and Adama Savadogo, who agreed to come and pose around the table and enjoy African food. Kristo Numpuby, for posing in some photos and for her priceless help and significant involvement. My son Swann, for posing in front of my camera on several occasions for this project, despite being super reluctant. I know it's hard to have a photographer for a mother!

To all the personalities who accepted my invitation to contribute to this book (Soro Solo, Mamani Keïta, Patrick Ruffino, Seydou Boro, Sandra Nkaké, Fred Ebami, Captain Alexandre, and Aïssé N'Diaye), who responded enthusiastically, and played along with the offbeat style of the portraits. Thanks in particular to Soro Solo, who was the first person I contacted and who replied with enthusiam; he really got the party started.

Isabelle Brouant, culinary stylist with a magic touch that makes any recipe look extra amazing!

Alfi, from the Keur Pigalle shop, David Cognon, from Holland Textiles (Sonna), and François Teytaud, Philippe Sonet, and Bertrand Sapin, from studio Imalliance, for lending us the Colorama backgrounds.

And of course, the whole team at Mango Editions, Aurélie Cazenave and Tatiana Delesalle, for believing in and investing in this book, which has already been met with much enthusiasm and positive feedback. Long may it last!

ISABELLE BROUANT

....

Thank you to CSAO for the tableware and furniture. For the tableware, I'd also like to thank Caravane, La boutique Keur, Jars, Maisons du Monde, Casa, Serax, Broste, and Pure.

In the portrait photos, the young man on p. 85 is wearing his own Benetton T-shirt.

The fabrics were loaned by Chef Anto from her brand Iwora, except for the fabric on p. 61 (wax Hitarget), p. 98 (wax G.T.P), and p. 119 (Dutch Wax Vlisco).

Thank you to Chef Anto for her good advice and help with the recipes.

Thank you Aline and for your love of Africa, which brought this wonderful project to life.

CHEF ANTO

This culinary work is the culmination of several years of passion, research, and work around our continent's produce and culinary traditions.

I would like to thank everyone who contributed in any way, shape, or form to the publication of this book, and in particular:

Aline Princet, culinary photographer, who had the original idea for this project and approached me to write the recipes.

Isabelle Brouant, culinary stylist, who understood all these recipes and made them look amazingly mouth-watering.

Aline and Isabelle, thank you for the magnificent photos, it was an absolute pleasure to work with you both. This book is stunning, thanks to you!

A big shout out to my grandmother Christine Jocktane, who we affectionately called "Titi," who left us at the beginning of the year, and so unfortunately is no longer with us to see the fruit of the culinary seeds she sowed in me when I was a little girl.

To my parents, Marcelle and Daniel Epoulou, who made the right decision in letting me follow my dreams of becoming a chef.

To my two men, Aaron and Nicolas, who have to put up with me every day and who always encourage me to follow my passion, the only way I will become a better mother and better wife.

To Kossi Modeste, my associate, the first person to have invested in me. In making me artistic director of the *Afro Cooking* magazine, you implicitly contributed to this cookbook becoming a reality.

To God, Master of time and circumstances, and source of my inspiration and passion. Thank you.

WHERE TO FIND INGREDIENTS

Ingredients can be sourced from African and Afro-Caribbean grocery stores, international markets, healthfood stores, and well-stocked supermarkets. You can also source ingredients from online retailers such as africamarketmn.com, goldcoastsupermarket.com, keitawestafricanmarket.com, as well as Amazon.com and Etsy.com.

First American edition published in 2022 by

Interlink Books
An imprint of Interlink Publishing Group, Inc.
46 Crosby Street
Northampton, Massachusetts 01060
www.interlinkbooks.com

Published simultaneously in the UK and Australia by Murdoch Books,
an imprint of Allen & Unwin
Originally published in French in 2019 by Mango Editions

Copyright © Mango 2019
American edition copyright © Interlink Publishing Group, Inc. 2022

Management: Guillaume Pô
Publishing director: Tatiana Delesalle
Publishing: Aurélie Cazenave assisted by Chloë Prestwich
Artistic director: Chloé Eve
Graphic design and layout: Séverine Charrier
Recipes: Chef Anto
Photos: Aline Princet
Recipe design: Isabelle Brouant
Wax prints on cover page and chapter opening pages: SONNA INTERNATIONAL

Publisher: Corinne Roberts
Translator: Nicola Thayil
English-language editor: Justine Harding
English-language designer: Susanne Geppert
Production Director: Lou Playfair

American edition publisher: Michel Moushabeck
American edition editor: Leyla Moushabeck
American edition proofreader: Jennifer McKenna

All rights reserved. No part of this publication may be reproduced, stored in a retrieval
system, or transmitted in any form or by any means, electronic, mechanical, photocopying,
recording, or otherwise, without the prior written permission of the publisher.

Library of Congress Cataloging-in-Publication
Data available

ISBN 978-1-62371-855-8

Printed and bound in China

TABLESPOON MEASURES: We have used 15 ml (3 teaspoon) tablespoon measures.

10 9 8 7 6 5 4 3 2 1

MIX
Paper from
responsible sources
FSC® C008047

The paper in this book is FSC® certified.
FSC® promotes environmentally responsible,
socially beneficial and economically viable
management of the world's forests.